# LITTLE
# CYCLONE

# LITTLE
# CYCLONE

## AIREY NEAVE

Biteback Publishing

This edition published in Great Britain in 2016 by
Biteback Publishing Ltd
Westminster Tower
3 Albert Embankment
London SE1 7SP
This edition copyright © The Airey Neave Trust 2013, 2016
Previous editions copyright © Airey Neave 1973, 1954

ISBN 978-1-84954-960-8

10 9 8 7 6 5 4 3 2 1

A CIP catalogue record for this book is available from the British Library.

Set in Garamond

Printed and bound in Great Britain by
CPI Group (UK) Ltd, Croydon CR0 4YY

MIX
Paper from
responsible sources
FSC
www.fsc.org
FSC® C020471

Dedicated to all the members of the Comet Line, and in particular the 156 men and women who sacrificed their lives to help Allied servicemen escape.

*The reason firm, the temperate will,*
*Endurance, foresight, strength and skill;*
*A perfect woman, nobly planned,*
*To warn, to comfort, and command;*
'SHE WAS A PHANTOM OF DELIGHT', WILLIAM WORDSWORTH

# Contents

# Introduction

When a 24-year-old Belgian girl arrived at the British Consulate in Bilbao in August 1941 with a young Scottish soldier she claimed to have brought down from Brussels through Occupied France and over the Pyrenees, she was denounced by MI6 as an obvious German plant. They soon changed their minds. Andrée De Jongh was dubbed 'the Little Cyclone' by her father because she was so determined it was impossible to ignore anything she said. She was inspired by Edith Cavell, the British nurse shot for espionage during the First World War, and after the Germans invaded Belgium in May 1940, she began nursing British soldiers trapped behind enemy lines. It was but a short step to emulating her heroine and setting up an escape line that would carry Allied servicemen through Occupied France and over the Pyrenees into neutral Spain.

Among the literally hundreds of Belgian, French and Basque agents who worked for the Comet Line, Andrée De Jongh was known only by her codename Dédée. MI6 initially dubbed her 'Postman', because she not only brought parcels, the servicemen she rescued – initially British soldiers trapped in Belgium, but later hundreds of escaped Allied prisoners of war or airmen shot down over occupied territory – she also brought letters, intelligence from inside Occupied Belgium and France.

The escape lines smuggling Allied servicemen out of Occupied Europe were run in London by MI9. It was ostensibly a department of military intelligence but in reality it was part of MI6, firmly under the control of the MI6 Assistant Chief, Claude Dansey. Interestingly, despite the British denial at the time of Edith Cavell's execution that she was a spy, Dansey and other senior members of MI6 justified their control over MI9 on the basis that Cavell's role as an intelligence agent was uncovered because of her other role in assisting Allied servicemen to escape. Andrée De Jongh truly was following in the footsteps of her heroine.

The author of this book, Airey Neave, who had himself escaped from Colditz and made his way home to Britain, was a leading member of MI9, along with Jimmy Langley, who later married Peggy van Lier, one of the heroines of this book. Neave wrote two books on his time running escape lines, one of them a more detailed account of the section's work, but it is *Little Cyclone* which is by far the more moving and exciting, relating the very human, real-life stories of the Belgian, Basque and French resistance members who risked their lives to spirit British and other Allied servicemen to freedom.

A true measure of the risk they faced can be judged from the list at the back of this book of the 156 members of the Comet Line who died as a result of their work helping Allied servicemen escape. They included Andrée De Jongh's father Frédéric, who ran the service from Brussels until his arrest in 1942. He was executed by firing squad. His daughter Andrée would become one of the Gestapo's most wanted targets. When she was finally arrested in January 1943, she was sent first to Ravensbrück concentration camp and then to Mauthausen.

She survived the camps. Eighty-eight of her colleagues did not, while a further four died of the dreadful effects of those camps shortly after being liberated. All of the people on that list, and indeed all of the members of the Comet Line to survive, are owed a huge debt, not only by the British and Allied forces they helped to rescue, but by all those who value freedom. This is a truly inspiring book.

*Michael Smith*
Editor of the Dialogue Espionage Classics
December 2012

# Foreword

When *Little Cyclone* was first published in 1954, I was a seven-year-old girl. Too young to understand. So I didn't read the book at the time, but I did hear the grown-ups around me talking about the girl whose father called her *le Petit Cyclone*. I heard how the Little Cyclone had spent the war doing the same dangerous things as my own father. How they helped Allied airmen to evade capture after their aircraft had been shot down by the *Boches* – the enemy who had invaded our country and treated our people so badly. How they crossed the Bidassoa River with Florentino, the Basque who would guide them across the Pyrenees to the safety of Spain. I was young, but I knew I was listening to a real human story. I could feel the action and feelings. It was fascinating.

From that moment on, the story of *le Réseau Comète*, the Comet Line, became a regular part of my life. Every year, different people, who always seemed to be great friends of my father, would arrive at our house from Great Britain, people like Airey Neave, Michael Creswell and James Langley and his wife Peggy, formerly Peggy van Lier of the Comet Line; from Canada, like the airman Angus McLean; from France, like the guides Yvonne and Robert Lapeyre; from all parts of Belgium. There was Tante Go, Michou, Monique, Jean-François, Jacques, Bernadette, Dédée, Albert… names that will be familiar to you when you have read this book. They were all there to do the same thing, talk about the same things, look at the same fragile, old papers which my father took out to show them year after year, after year. Each year telling a different, real, living story, remembering together events that seemed to them always to be a good memory, albeit tinged with sadness. Then they would sip a drop, or sometimes more, of whisky or cognac. Every year from the end of the war onward, the members of the *Amicale Comète* came to Brussels to remember and to celebrate the rescue of people, of countries, of life, in the name of the freedom they fought for throughout the years of war. They all had the same spirit: generosity, dedication to helping others and saving others' lives; fighting without weapons, without killing. As described by Jean-François Nothomb, the head of *le Réseau Comète* after the arrest of the initiator and embodiment of the spirit of the escape line, Dédée De Jongh:

> In their efforts to rescue others and in the strength of their
> love, the members of Comète were armed only with their
> courage and their belief in the value of freedom.

The Comet Line was a chain of people from different countries, from different backgrounds, of different beliefs, religions, lifestyles, and yet it was a family. There were 2,000, 3,000… nobody will ever know exactly how many. We are still discovering new names of that huge network, each one linked secretly to the others.

‡

The Comet Line lasted from August 1941 to the end of 1944. After the war, the *Amicale Comète* preserved their bonds and memories until 2001. In 2005, I heard that there was a '*Comète* Walk' being organised in the Pyrenees and I went. I wanted to live the famous Bidassoa of my childhood and the world of Florentino. I discovered much more. The spirit of the Comet Line was still alive, with no boundaries of either time or place. So many different people from every continent, and all there with the same feelings and desire: to share and to discover and to share some more. All were so different but each had their own fascinating link to *Comète*. One was there because, assisted by the Line, his father had crossed the Pyrenees to reach the United Kingdom. Another was looking for information about his uncle who crashed and was helped to escape. One was following his mother's footsteps to write the story of her war as part of the Comet Line and her escape after she was 'burned' (betrayed). Another was a nephew of Florentino. One was a son of a fisherman who brought the escapers fish. Another was the son of someone in MI9. There was a historian explaining what happened. Volunteers from the whole area were helping. There was a *Sardinade*, a typical southern French festivity in which fresh sardines are barbecued and eaten. People were singing the folk songs. I found myself sitting next to the flag-bearer of the old *Amicale Comète*. He told me:

> I am the son of the plumber who helped in guiding, lodg-
> ing. You too [are the daughter of one of the line]. We are the
> *Comète* young generation. All the veterans are getting old. We
> should be the fresh, new troops to relieve those who fought
> before us. The spirit of *Comète* is extending naturally because

it is a universal and eternal message. We have a duty to pass it on to the next generation.

So, in December 2005, the *Comète Kinship Belgium* was set up with the written agreement of Andrée De Jongh, the 'Little Cyclone', by now the Countess Andrée De Jongh. Very quickly, there were more than 150 members. We ensured that the annual meeting of the remaining veterans of the *Amicale Comète* continued, welcoming all the airmen who wanted to come back to Brussels with their families, friends, helpers. Every year, on a Sunday, a memorial service takes place in the Basilica of Koekelberg, in front of a *Comète* stained-glass window and the RAF Chapel. Then there is a family lunch for everyone in the *Maison des Ailes* (the Belgian equivalent of the RAF Club). On the Saturday before the ceremony, there is a visit to a place of interest or remembrance. The atmosphere is convivial and simple, but strong. The date of the ceremony is chosen to be close to 20 October, to commemorate the day in 1943 when eleven *Comète* helpers were shot by the Germans in the *Tir national*. We produce the *Comète-Infos*, a newsletter which not only provides news of what is happening but also retraces the history of the Comet Line with testimonies, research and analysis. We realise more and more that Dédée De Jongh and her Comet Line have become legends. Somebody told me not long ago, 'The Comet Line will never stop existing.' I think their spirit of generosity and the attention they gave to other people and to the fight for freedom have found a place in people's hearts and that across the world there are people who believe, like them, that everybody has a right to live. We believe that the spirit that drove the Comet Line still, somehow, exists even among the conflicts which take place across the world, that it is a strong spirit, a spirit worth promulgating.

Dédée De Jongh received the title of Countess from the King of Belgium in her eighties. She was awarded a lot of very high decorations from different countries. Even when she was young, she was already a 'Little Cyclone'. She made things happen around her. At twenty-four, when war was declared, she immediately began working as a nurse in a hospital in Bruges where she met soldiers wanting to go home. Her path in life was already set. She would help them find their way home. Determined, enthusiastic, positive, showing no fear of anything, Dédée found the people who would help her fulfil her destiny. Her obvious strength radiated from her entire body. So much strength showed in her face that she instilled strength, willingness and confidence in all around her. As many Comet escapers testified, the spirit of Comet derived from 'the Little Cyclone'. She emanated such positive energy that it rallied every other bit of positive energy around her to her cause.

The republication of this book is a tribute to all those who fight or have fought against war.

I am involved in the *Comète* association because life gave me the opportunity to do it, and I didn't hesitate for long. My father entered the Line at a time when he was trying to reach the United Kingdom. At the beginning of 1942, he met a friend (Albert Greindl) who said to him, 'There is better work to do here.' He didn't hesitate long. As a very communicative and enthusiastic person, he knew a lot of people here and there. He found people in whom he had confidence to inform him of an escaper looking for a way to evade, to lodge, dress, feed, or to produce false papers. My father was a guide, helping people who were on the run move safely across Belgium and down through France to Paris, which he knew because of his French mother. He helped for eight months, then had to escape himself and walked to safety along the route that went across the Bidassoa River, guided by Florentino. In Great Britain, he trained as a secret agent and was sent to the area of France around Reims to help those people who were being extracted by Lysander aircraft. He was also in contact with the Comet Line representatives in Paris. He had to escape a second time and then finished his war in the Belgian SAS Parachute Squadron. Now, one of his grandchildren is interested in the Comet Line and has been a flag-bearer with the *Comète* standard. The Little Cyclone's spirit of generosity and attention to others will never die.

*Comtesse Brigitte d'Oultremont*
*Président, Comète Kinship Belgium*
Gentinnes, February 2013

# Author's Note

The characters in this book are real. They were the leaders of an underground organisation in which hundreds of ordinary folk in Belgium and France played a part. Those who still live seek no publicity, but they are willing that the story should be told to keep alive the spirit which fired them.

In writing the book I have had the unique advantage of their friendship. I am particularly grateful to Suzanne, Dédée's sister, for reading my manuscript and allowing me to make use of her book *Comete: Ligne d'évasion*. I cannot name all the members of Comet who helped me with details of their epic story, but I must mention Madame Robert Aylé, Madame Elvire De Greef GM (Tante Go) and all her family, Baronne Jean Greindl (Nemo's widow), Florentino, Mrs J. M. Langley MBE (Peggy), Madame Maréchal, Madame Claude Courtois (Elsie), Mademoiselle Elvire Morelle, MBE, Monsieur Jean Naus, Frère Jean-François Nothomb DSO (Franco), and Count Georges d'Oultremont, MBE, MM.

Mr Albert Edward Johnson, MBE (the 'B' Johnson of this tale), to the great grief of all members of the Comet Line, died in February of this year. I wish to thank his widow, Mrs Wendy Johnson, for the help she has given me in recording his courage and devotion.

I also wish to thank Mr Charles Sutton, Mr Brinsley Ford

MBE, and Mr Arthur S. Dean, lately HM Consul at Bilbao, for all their trouble and advice.

But I owe the greatest debt of all to the incomparable Dédée herself – Mademoiselle Andrée De Jongh GM – who told me her story.

*Airey Neave*
August 1954

# Prologue

On a hot afternoon in August 1941, Little Cyclone swept into the British Consulate at Bilbao. She had marched all the way from Brussels on a mission which no one had thought possible. The overworked Consul rose courteously from his chair and faced the young girl, with no sign on his face of the suspicion which he felt about her.

'Mademoiselle Andrée De Jongh?'

The girl nodded. Her eyes did not waver under his stern gaze.

'It is safer to call me Dédée,' she said.

The Consul laid down his pipe and looked closely at his visitor.

'I have heard about you from our Consul at San Sebastián, tell me your story.'

'I am a Belgian, and I have come all the way from Brussels,' she said. 'I have brought you two Belgians who want to fight for the Allies, and a Scottish soldier. We left Brussels last week and crossed the Pyrenees two nights ago.'

The Consul looked warily at the small figure, dressed in a simple blouse and skirt and flat shoes with white ankle socks. He tapped his pipe meditatively.

'Where is the Scotsman?' he asked.

'He is downstairs with the two Belgians.' The girl smiled.

'How long did your journey take?'

'I have told you. About a week.'

There was an incredulous tone in his voice:

'How did you get over the Pyrenees?'

The girl's blue eyes shone with triumph.

'I have friends near Bayonne who were able to get a Basque guide. He brought us through without difficulty. It was a good trip.'

Her hands clutched the side of the leather armchair and, leaning forward eagerly, she continued:

'There are many British soldiers and airmen hidden in Brussels, most of them survivors from Dunkirk. I can bring them through to you here if you will let me. My father and I have already formed an escape line all the way from Brussels to St Jean de Luz. With money, we can find guides to cross the mountains.'

The Consul did not betray his unbelief.

'How old are you?' he shot at her.

'I am twenty-five.'

The Consul noticed her bare arms. They were slim and delicate. Her face, without make-up, was intelligent. Her mouth and nose were not beautiful, but determined and arresting. There was an eagerness and power about her that impressed him.

'But you – you are a young girl. You are not going to cross the Pyrenees again?'

'But, yes. I am as strong as a man. Girls attract less attention in the frontier zone than men. The Basque guide, Thomas, I have found, will take me back. With your help I can bring through more Englishmen. I beg of you to let me.'

The Consul turned his impassive face to the window and for several moments there was no sound but the whirr and rattle of the trams outside.

'We are more interested in British servicemen, of course,' he said.

The young woman laughed.

'Naturally. My father and I have agreed that we shall concentrate on bringing through as many trained fighting men as we can. All we need is money to pay our guides, and for feeding and housing the men on the long route from Brussels to Bilbao.'

'How much does it cost you to bring a man from Brussels?' said the Consul.

He looked at her searchingly. He still doubted that this slip of a girl had really crossed the Pyrenees on foot. It was an arduous journey, and he had never heard of anyone except smugglers attempting it before. The ugly thought came to him that the Germans might have sent her. Could she be a stool pigeon? And yet, she looked too innocent to be a traitor.

She answered without hesitation:

'6,000 Belgian francs from Brussels to St Jean de Luz.'

The Consul grimly pencilled the figure on his blotting pad.

'That should be about 2,021 pesetas. What about the mountain guides?'

'1,400 pesetas.'

He stood up and looked fixedly at her:

'That seems very expensive.'

'I agree, but the guides are nervous of taking Allied soldiers through occupied territory, particularly the coastal zone.'

The Consul was silent for a moment, writing at his desk. There was the heady smell of good tobacco. The girl waited tensely.

'I must refer all this to my superiors. When do you think you can come back with another party?'

The girl was delighted.

'In three or four weeks' time.'

'Then bring three more men with you.'

The Consul held out his hand. There were many refugees to whom he must attend. He must dismiss this strange visitor and hope that in fact she would return in three or four weeks with more rescued men.

'*Au revoir, Mademoiselle.*'

'*Au revoir, Monsieur le Consul.*'

The Little Cyclone walked swiftly from the room and down the stairs. Her disappointment at this cautious reception mingled with pleasure at the prospect of establishing an escape route that became the famous Comet Line.

Private Cromar of the 1st Gordons, a survivor of St Valéry, stood waiting outside with two young Belgians. They made a modest group, disguised in rough working clothes. Their faces revealed their joy at the first exquisite taste of liberty.

The girl shook their hands. Private Cromar held hers for a moment.

'Goodbye, Colin.'

'Good luck, Miss,' he said. 'And God bless you!'

She waved to the three men and was gone, like some kindly sprite. She was soon lost in the crowd of office workers, hurrying home. It was still very hot and the dust of the streets of Bilbao was in her eyes and throat.

The tram to San Sebastián gave time for reflection as she gazed out over the shimmering sea. Why had the Consul seemed so unimpressed? She felt a sharp pang of disappointment. She wondered if the British suspected her of working for the Germans. Did they think that she was being used to bring enemy agents to neutral territory? No, that could not be true, otherwise the shrewd Consul would never have allowed her to return to France. For a moment there were tears in her eyes. Then she remembered her triumphant conquest of the mountains.

Dédée did not know that, despite his early misgivings, the Consul was already won over. He had made up his mind to obtain the support of the British Foreign Office for her plan. His kindly encouragement was to be of the greatest value to the Comet Line.

She resolved to go back to Brussels and tell her father, Frédéric De Jongh, that what had seemed impossible had been achieved. There had been faint hearts among her friends who sheltered soldiers and airmen in Belgium, who had said that there could never be an escape route all the way to Spain.

The Comet Line was her dream. In the next few months she created it. It became the greatest escape route of all. In its three years of life, 800 Allied airmen and soldiers were saved from captivity and returned to England to fight again.

She thought of her early life as a student designing posters, and of training to be a nurse. Posters! She looked at her fine hands and smiled.

In 1940, war had come and offered her adventure. There was the hospital in Belgium where she had worked as a nurse among wounded British soldiers. There were the prisoners in Germany to whom she had sent parcels. Their helplessness had moved her deeply.

The invasion of the Germans had released her from a humdrum existence. As a young girl, she had loved from afar the great French pilot, Mermoz, who had flown for thousands of miles over uncharted land and sea. His brave story thrilled her. It helped her in her decision to aid Allied soldiers and airmen, hiding in Belgium.

Early in 1941 she began to gather friends around her, who agreed to house and feed young Belgians and servicemen of the Allies who wished to escape to England. Her foremost comrade in this dangerous work was her father, Frédéric De Jongh. In 1915 he had found inspiration in the sacrifice of Edith Cavell. A generation later it was the spirit of his own daughter which fired him.

He liked to think of her as 'Little Cyclone', the name he had given her as a child. It marked her lively nature and high spirits. She was always rushing to and fro. But to her friends she was Dédée, the affectionate name given to girls named Andrée in Belgium. It was as Dédée that she was known to hundreds of members of the Comet Line which she created. To the British Foreign Office she became the 'Postman', who delivered secret parcels at Bilbao.

It was a misfortune to be a woman, she thought.

'But', she said to herself, 'I can walk as far and as fast as any man.'

She laughed with pleasure as she recalled that night of summer a few weeks earlier. With a young countryman named Arnold Deppé, she had set out with her first party of fugitives from Brussels to the Spanish frontier. This was the pioneer effort which led to the formation of the Comet Line.

## Chapter One

# Dédée

She took with her ten Belgians, wanted by the Gestapo, and a plump, middle-aged Englishwoman in a Panama hat. Miss Richards, as she was called, though Dédée never knew her real name, was threatened with internment.

In Brussels the spring sun shone warmly. Arnold and Dédée, dividing their forces, split up the party, and boarded different compartments in the train for Lille. As the train, packed with passengers, left Brussels, Dédée felt her heart beat wildly. This was her first bold stroke. Would it succeed?

Miss Richards evidently considered that a clandestine voyage to the Spanish frontier should be treated like any other journey. Her luggage consisted, despite the entreaties of Dédée and Arnold, of a substantial suitcase, a handbag and an umbrella. The thought of crossing the Pyrenees on foot did not deter her from regarding this experience as similar to any other form of travel.

Miss Richards sat, pink and indignant, in the corner of her compartment. Dédée, on her first adventure, thought how easy it all seemed. They would have to leave the train at Quiévrain and cross from Belgium into France. Then would come two more train journeys and the crossing of the River Somme by boat at Corbie, near Amiens. Arnold had chosen the crossing place near Corbie. With the aid of Nenette, a farmer's wife, a boat had been hidden among the reeds on the east bank of the river.

They left the train at Quiévrain, and their false identity cards, forged by hand, were not examined. Then they tramped through a meadow to avoid further controls, borne down with Miss Richards's luggage, to Blanc-Misseron to take the train to Lille.

The sky was very blue as Dédée strode cheerfully beside Arnold, the others following.

After two hours in a local train they reached Lille and changed for Corbie, where they stopped for a meal. At sunset the escapers and their guides in single file made their way towards the bank of the Somme. There was the sharp snap of twigs as Arnold, leading the party, forged towards the river.

Arnold, leaving them crouching in a copse, moved forward to search for the boat hidden by Nenette, who was waiting on the far bank. It was now dark and there was a faint red glow among the trees. Groping forward, Arnold stumbled on a group of holiday-makers round a campfire. Their tents had been pitched in a clearing a few yards from the spot where the boat was concealed. Arnold, frustrated, clenched his fists. It would be impossible to guide the escapers past the campers or the German patrols without attracting attention.

Arnold returned to the copse.

'There is nothing for it, Dédée,' he whispered. 'We must swim across.'

Miss Richards's white Panama, faintly outlined against the sky, betrayed her still-indignant presence. The Belgians were whispering nervously.

'Six of the men and Miss Richards are non-swimmers,' said Dédée. 'Arnold, we must ferry them over. We want a length of wire or rope and something like a lifebelt.'

Arnold disappeared again to search for means of improvising a ferry. There was still time before daylight to find the necessary materials from neighbouring farms.

Dédée crept silently to the river, knelt beside it and peered across. The water flowed calmly by, leaving a black sludge on the bank. The breeze blew softly through the rushes. Dédée looked towards a cluster of tall trees on the far side.

There Nenette must be anxiously waiting, unaware of what had gone wrong. Suddenly, Dédée flung herself into the brambles, as the light of a bicycle lamp came silently towards her along the towpath. Its beams swung from right to left, and cast strange shadows. As it passed her, she glimpsed the shape of a German helmet. Slowly, terribly slowly, the light vanished along the bank.

The party, crouching by the river, awaited Arnold's return. Dédée had already formed her plan, which was to run a line across the river from trees on either bank so that the men and Miss Richards, clinging to a floating object, could be towed across.

At two in the morning, someone hoarsely whispered Dédée's name. Arnold was back with a length of good wire and the inflated inner tube of a motor tyre.

After a short conference Arnold fastened the wire round a tree. Then came another lamp winking along the towpath. Everybody fell flat until it had passed.

When all was clear Arnold splashed into the water and quietly swam across the river, uncoiling the line. Five minutes passed and there was a tugging on the wire – the signal for Dédée to start sending passengers across on the rubber tyre.

The first to cross, a stout, panting youth, floundered through the oozing mud and clambered on to the tyre, desperately embracing the line. Dédée, knowing that he could not swim, tore off her tartan skirt and blouse and waded into the water. She swam easily across the river, propelling the rubber tyre and the fat youth in front of her. Her vision was obscured by the large behind of her ungainly passenger. She knew that she had reached the other side when her feet touched the mud and she saw the stout youth scramble forward. She swam back to the east bank to collect her next passenger.

There was little current, and Dédée, untiring and excited, swam the river to and fro eleven times. The Belgians, who could swim, crossed alone and were hustled, shivering, by Nenette to her home 100 yards away. It was a dangerous operation. The splashing they made caused Dédée anxiety, for at any moment another German patrol might appear.

But in spite of the danger there was one delicious moment. Dédée, years afterwards, could never think of the crossing of Miss Richards without chuckling. Her suitcase, which had encumbered the party, was left among the trees, partly emptied, and a pile of tweed skirts and underclothes and shoes was ferried across on a large piece of wood. In spite of her protests, Miss Richards was advised to take off her skirt in order that she should arrive on the other bank with dry clothes. Dédée, in her impatience, nearly tore it off her. Miss Richards took it off and stood, revealed in startling white bloomers. Even at a distance, they formed a ghostly patch of brightness. Picked out in the beam of German cycle lamp, they would be an easy target.

'Now you must take *them* off, *Mademoiselle*,' said the anxious Dédée.

'What!'

'They will be seen by the Germans on the towpath.'

'I can't help it,' spluttered Miss Richards. 'I refuse to take them off.'

There was a faint snigger in the trees.

Dédée, having angrily launched Miss Richards on the tyre, swam a side-stroke, half pushing, half pulling her across. She soon changed from this uncomfortable manoeuvre and propelled Miss Richards from behind. This caused Miss Richards to tip forward. Her Panama hat vanished into the darkness and all that Dédée could see was her vast posterior. The tyre began to slip and bulge out from under Miss Richards. There was an anxious few seconds while she was hoisted back on to the tyre.

Dédée was becoming weary after several journeys. Her legs ached and the water seemed bitterly cold.

'Oh, God, look!' said Miss Richards, moaning.

Another bicycle lamp appeared on the towpath.

'Slip into the water and hang on to the tyre,' whispered Dédée.

There was a splash and Miss Richards slid into the river. The two women clung together until the lamplight was gone. Then Miss Richards, wet, panting and terrified, was hauled by Arnold up the bank.

It had taken an hour and a half for the whole party to cross the river. Dédée had been in the water all this time. As she lay exhausted on an old sofa in Nenette's farmhouse, she thought of the night's experience as something she would never forget. Exciting, and at times hilarious, as it had been, everyone had been in danger. But a lesson had been learned. Next time there must be no mistake about the boat. This first crossing of the Somme was a vital landmark in the history of the Comet Line.

## Chapter Two

## Tante Go

On the road from St Jean de Luz to Bayonne is a village called Anglet. A narrow lane leads to a drab, grey villa with a view of the distant mountains and below them the sparkling blue of the bay of St Jean de Luz. It was to this inconspicuous place that Dédée came when she returned from the British consulate in Bilbao. It was here that, with Arnold Deppé, she had brought Miss Richards and the ten Belgians six weeks before. Here, too, she had rested in the warm southern weather before she set out on her first march over the Pyrenees. Three weeks had passed before she found herself once more in the shabby sweep of drive in front of the villa.

She knocked on the door. It was opened by a slight, round-faced woman who wore a striped dress and sandals. Her auburn hair was cut short. She had prominent, fierce grey eyes tinged with green. Her age was difficult to guess. She looked, at the most, thirty-five. As she stood at the door, no one could have doubted that here was a strong and vital character. Her name was Elvire De Greef, alias Tante Go. Her strange pseudonym derived from the original password used by visitors to the villa at Anglet and recalled a lamented pet dog called 'Gogo'.

*'Gogo est mort.'*

Tante Go, a Belgian like Dédée, had worked before the war in the offices of a well-known Belgian newspaper. Her husband, Fernand, had been in business in Brussels. They had lived with their two children, Freddy and Janine, at the villa at Anglet since the summer of 1940. When the Germans invaded Belgium, they set out with their children for Bordeaux to take ship to England to serve the Allies. But in the scrimmage which followed the collapse of the French, there was no room for them. For days they wandered disconsolately in search of shelter. At length they found the empty villa and became its tenants. They lived there all the war and gave magnificent service to the Comet Line.

Tante Go, as she was known from Brussels to Bilbao, was the driving force of this courageous family. Early in 1941 Arnold Deppé had come to the villa as a messenger from Dédée and her father. He had known the De Greefs in happier days in Belgium. He now besought them to help him find a guide who would take young men, who wished to escape to England, over the Pyrenees.

Tante Go was delighted. She was bored by life at the villa. Freddy and Janine, aged eighteen and seventeen, were able to continue their studies in Bayonne. Her husband, Fernand, had become interpreter to the German headquarters at Anglet. She therefore pledged her aid, and immediately took charge of operations in the Spanish frontier zone. With Arnold, she searched in the underworld of St Jean de Luz and Ciboure and found the smuggler, Thomas, who later guided Dédée on her first journey to Bilbao at an exorbitant price.

When Arnold returned to Belgium to report to Dédée and bring down Miss Richards and the ten Belgians, Tante Go busied herself with finding 'safe' houses where parties could shelter before they crossed to Spain. She was vigorous and brave, a great organiser. In a short time, a marshalling point for fugitives had been established in the neighbourhood of Anglet, where Tante Go, bicycling furiously from house to house, recruited new helpers every day.

Tante Go and her husband and children were well qualified for underground warfare. Fernand De Greef, tall and dark and youthful in appearance, readily accepted the spirited lead of his wife as Commander-in-Chief in the south. He became her devoted assistant in the task of building an escape organisation. He was well placed for this purpose in the *Kommandantur* at Anglet.

His job as interpreter gave him excellent opportunities to aid her. Before Dédée returned from her first visit to Spain, he had begun to purloin in blank the identity cards which were essential for bona fide travellers in Occupied France. He had also access to special passes and *certificats de domicil* required for visitors to the forbidden zone established by the Germans along the Atlantic coast. These precious documents Fernand stealthily removed in small quantities from the office where he worked.

As the part he played in the history of the Comet Line grew in importance, he became known as 'L'Oncle', as befitted the husband of 'La Tante'. (From the earliest days real names were never used.) 'La Tante' was forceful and commanding; 'L'Oncle', modest and ingenious, was the perfect counterpart.

The German officers of the *Kommandantur* were ignorant of these formidable and cunning enemies in their midst. With an obliging smile, L'Oncle daily performed his delicate task of billeting enemy troops, of whom there were several thousand in the area. He took the opportunity, as he visited the headquarters of German units, to steal official stamps. In time he acquired a substantial store of identity documents and forms, from which he supplied the branches of the escape line in Paris and Brussels. He was able, by virtue of a special order from the *Kommandantur*, to pass freely in the streets at night and undertake many a vital mission for Tante Go.

The amiable L'Oncle and his wife spent the whole war in the service of Comet. Despite frequent alarms and occasions when they were detained and questioned by the Gestapo, they saw the liberation of France. They were in it at the beginning. They saw it through to the end. Their son, Freddy, after helping his mother by travelling at night with urgent messages in German uniform, escaped to England in 1943. Janine, their daughter, remained with them until 6 June 1944, the day when she crossed the Pyrenees to reach Britain.

Tante Go was ruthless and energetic. Early in her remarkable career she began to operate freely on the black market. Her purpose was to obtain good food for the escapers, which would give them courage and strength in their ordeal. It was a sound policy. A tired and hungry British airman or soldier might lose his nerve when confronted by a *gendarme* or frontier guard. Excellent steaks were cooked at the villa by her mother-in-law, known as 'Bobonne'.

The black market and the resistance movement were closely linked. The possession of rare delicacies and cigarettes became a fruitful source of corruption of German sentries and even of higher officials. To this game Tante Go applied herself with natural guile. Day after day she bicycled with Janine to the houses of her contacts in Bayonne, Anglet, Biarritz and St Jean de Luz. In cafés and *bistros* were numerous smugglers of her acquaintance. By dealing in black-market goods, she lulled suspicion of her activities. It enabled her to conduct her rescue work under the very noses of the Germans.

'L'Oncle' and the children were the pioneers of Tante Go's system. She was their undisputed leader. From the first she was the chief in the south, owing allegiance only to Little Cyclone.

At the door of the villa, Tante Go and Dédée embraced.

'How wonderful that you are safely back from Spain,' cried Tante Go. 'We were becoming anxious.'

Together the two women walked to the lawn in front of the villa and, sitting in deckchairs, talked in the sun.

'What happened, Dédée?' asked Tante Go.

'The British were not encouraging, but they have agreed that I should take another party to Bilbao in three weeks' time.'

'Well done. I never thought you would make it. After what happened to Miss Richards and the ten Belgians, I had almost given up hope.'

'Have you any more news?'

'No. I only know what Thomas has already told us. They were all arrested by *carabineros* as soon as they arrived in Spain. They are probably in the concentration camp of Miranda.'

'I was furious,' said Dédée. 'What was the use of our raising money to hide and feed people who wanted to escape, if they only finished in Spanish concentration camps? It made me determined to go and see the British and arrange for them to take the men over on the Spanish side.'

'Did they agree?' said Tante Go.

'Oh, yes, but I hope it won't be necessary for me to take them all the way to Bilbao. I hope to persuade the British to collect them in San Sebastián.'

'What about money?'

Dédée laughed heartily.

'The Consul would only pay me for the Scotsman! I asked to be paid only for bringing the men from Brussels and the cost of a guide over the frontier. We must remain independent of the British.'

Tante Go nodded. She noticed the defiant tilt of Dédée's nose and remembered a conversation with her three weeks before. She had been anxious for this young girl setting out on so perilous a journey.

'Thomas will never take a girl,' she had said.

'You wait and see, Tante.'

And now the older woman asked:

'However did you get Thomas to take you?'

'Oh, I persuaded him to let me walk with him in the hills. You see, my legs are very strong. I used to swim a lot and go for long walks in the Ardennes. He was astonished that I could keep up with him. Then he gave way. But he is much too expensive. We need a cheaper guide.'

There was the sound of tyres crunching on the gravel and a slender figure in white shorts jumped from her bicycle and ran towards them.

Janine De Greef was seventeen and very pretty. She had rich blonde hair and brown eyes. Had there been no escape line, she might have spent the next four years like any girl of her age. But from the moment when the Little Cyclone came to their door and cast her spell over them, the family of De Greef were destined to play a skilled and dangerous game.

Janine lay beside them on the lawn as Tante Go said to Dédée:

'I am afraid we have no news of Arnold.'

Dédée frowned.

'He is almost certainly arrested. I think they got him at the station at Lille. At Brussels we split up into two parties. I took the train to Valenciennes with the Scotsman and the two Belgians. I had no trouble. Even the boat was at Corbie with Nenette in attendance.'

'You did not have to swim, at any rate!' said Tante Go.

'But that would not have mattered. If only I could find out what happened to the others!' Dédée sighed.

'I had a rendezvous with Arnold at a café at Corbie. We waited there for hours. There was no sign of him, so I left the three men with Nenette and returned to Lille to look for him.

'I went to the station, but there were too many *gendarmes* about. Then I went to the cafés in Lille where we have contacts. I could not find him anywhere.'

There was a hint of desperation in her voice.

'So I had to come on alone with my three "children", but I am still hoping for news from Belgium.'

While Dédée and Tante Go talked in the sunlight, a young man appeared with a lawnmower and, assisted by Janine, began to mow the grass. He was an Englishman named Albert Edward Johnson, known to everyone in that exotic group as 'B'.

Dédée was sad at the disappearance of Arnold. Already the earliest members of the Comet Line had encountered danger. Yet, undaunted, they decided to seek a new guide instead of the rapacious Thomas.

They sat talking till the sun began to set behind the dark primeval barrier of the Pyrenees, which Dédée was so often to cross in the coming year. The crickets sang in the fields. 'B' Johnson was oiling the lawnmower. 'L'Oncle' was quietly listening to the two women, while Janine, with the sunset on her golden hair, sat cross-legged beside him.

Suddenly everyone was alert. There were soft footsteps in the drive. A low whistle in the dusk.

It was Dédée who spoke first:

'Charlie Morelle!'

A smiling, fair-haired, young man, carrying a suitcase, walked up to them. He shook hands.

'Have you seen my parents, Charlie?' asked Dédée impatiently.

'Yes, certainly. But I am afraid my news is not good.' His face momentarily lost its cheerful expression. 'Arnold was arrested at the station at Lille with the whole of his party. Dédée, the Gestapo is looking for you. You cannot go back to Belgium!'

## Chapter Three

# Paul

While Dédée was in Spain, the Gestapo called one evening at the home of her parents at No. 73 Avenue Émile Verhaeren in the Schaerbeek district of Brussels. A grey Opel car came down the street at dusk.

The street has an air of wan gentility. It is modest and respectable. There is nothing grave or gay in its atmosphere, only restraint. It seems far removed from high adventure. Yet behind the lace curtains of No. 73 there breathed the very spirit of resistance to Hitler.

Their neighbours in wartime little suspected the fires which burned within. Today, looking back over the years, they can remember Frédéric De Jongh, Dédée's father, walking each morning to the school in the Place Gauchard of which he was head master. They can remember his spare figure at dusk on a summer evening long ago, crossing the roadway with Dédée and her elder sister, Suzanne, and hearing their laughter as they entered No. 73.

In 1941, Frédéric De Jongh was fifty-eight. He had the look of one used to study, and his eyes appeared short-sighted behind thick spectacles. Yet there was strength in his scholarly features. His chin and mouth were resolute and his grey hair, brushed firmly back, revealed a straight, broad forehead.

He was a dreamer who believed in human goodness. He

was unwilling to believe the worst even of Germans, but his country's surrender in 1940 had shocked him deeply. On the day of the fatal news he came back to the Avenue Émile Verhaeren in tears. He was soon determined to expunge his sense of shame. At the end of 1940 he had already made contact with several British survivors of Dunkirk, hiding in Brussels. He became known by the alias of Paul and, with a few friends, raised funds to feed and clothe the men, always referring to them as '*mes enfants*'. It was an apt expression of his feelings and of those of his daughter.

The evening of the Gestapo's visit was still and warm. The Opel stopped sharply at No. 73. Neighbours of Paul, as they sat at their doors or strolled in the sunset, watched a big, blond German ring the bell. A shiver went through the watchers, as if a chill breeze of death was blowing down the street. It was the first time they had seen the Gestapo.

Two Germans stood impatiently at the door. They were tall and carried briefcases. Their felt hats shaded cruel, blue eyes; each had a fixed expression of annoyance and disdain.

There was a muffled sound within and Paul, breathless, opened the door. He had only had a few seconds to hide some blank identity cards and money.

'Frédéric De Jongh?'

Paul nodded. He was pushed roughly inside and, with the two men of the Gestapo, climbed the dark stairs. The boots of the Germans made a hollow, ominous sound. They crossed a landing and entered a demure sitting room overlooking the street. In the evening shadows sat Dédée's mother, Madame De Jongh, and her sister-in-law, Tante Nini.

The Germans seemed to fill the room. They still wore their hats, but bowed with ungraceful curtness to the two ladies. One took out a notebook and sat at the family dining table covered by a green baize cloth. The other began to fire questions at Paul.

'Where is your daughter Andrée?'

Despite his beating heart, the schoolmaster studied them short-sightedly. Both of them were gauche and young. A clumsy interrogation ensued.

Paul shrugged his shoulders.

'She left home months ago. Young girls – you understand,' he sighed.

It became clear that the Gestapo had a complete description of her.

Paul had heard of the arrest of Arnold. Someone in his party, arrested at the station at Lille, must have talked.

He thought momentarily of Dédée, dressed in the youthful costume which she wore when travelling on her dangerous mission. She would be difficult to catch, for she could go unnoticed in a crowd. Like many an unusual personality, she shone at a moment of challenge and then receded to a modest corner. It seemed that the Gestapo had only faintly grasped the existence of an escape organisation.

Of his own activity they appeared to know little.

'What is your occupation?'

'Schoolmaster.'

'Do you go to the school every morning?'

The questioning dragged on. The German voices grated in the respectable front room. Madame De Jongh, Tante Nini and Suzanne, Dédée's elder sister, were sharply questioned. Not once did they falter in their faith. The family was committed to Dédée from the start. Who could have restrained this whirlwind girl?

They pretended to know nothing except that she had left home weeks ago. After an hour, the Gestapo, fretful but half satisfied, left to go.

'Nowadays one cannot keep track of what young people do,' said Paul.

The Germans smiled sardonically.

He followed them down the stairs, and when the door was closed behind them, sat on the bottom step to wipe his brow.

The night passed and in the Avenue Émile Verhaeren there was a rattle of shutters opening on a rainy morning. Charlie Morelle, bareheaded and in a raincoat, walked unconcernedly along the street. He was thirty, and a Frenchman to the fingertips. His blond, curling hair receded slightly from his forehead. His face was sharp and quizzical; his long, humorous nose gave character and wit to all his features. He bore a strong resemblance to Dédée's hero, the legendary French pilot, Mermoz.

In 1940, when a lieutenant in a French cavalry regiment, he had been taken prisoner by the Germans. He had escaped on foot to Belgium and had sheltered in the house of a certain Madame Maréchal of the Avenue Voltaire, a friend of Dédée and her father. Dédée supplied him with false papers to reach his home at Valenciennes in safety.

When Arnold and his party disappeared, Dédée turned to his gay and friendly character for aid. On the evening of her vain search for Arnold in Lille, she arrived at Charlie's house at Valenciennes, remembering that he had promised to help her if ever she needed him.

Her face was white and serious.

'Charlie, I need your help badly. Will you do something for me?'

'*De tout mon cœur*, Dédée,' he said. 'You can count on me and my wife and Elvire, my sister. We will help you in every way. What do you want?'

'Please go to 73, Avenue Émile Verhaeren at Schaerbeek in Brussels and find my father, Frédéric De Jongh, who is known as Paul. Perhaps he will have news of what has happened. Tell him that I must go south with my three men, as I cannot leave them for long at Corbie.'

'Do not worry, Dédée. I will find out everything I can.'

'Do tell my father to be careful. He is really too old for this kind of thing, and he has his school to look after. When you have got all the information you can, go to this address at Anglet, near Bayonne.' She gave him the address of Tante Go. 'I am going on alone.'

Charlie looked at her with admiration.

A few days later, Charlie, equipped with false papers, took the train to Brussels. He felt once more the tingling excitement which he had known on his escape. His eyes were expectant. His big nose was ready to scent danger. He called it his '*pifomètre*'.

He rang the bell of No. 73.

The door was opened warily by Paul. His face was strained and tired.

Charlie smiled: 'I wish to speak to Paul.'

'Who are you?'

'I come from Dédée. My name is Charlie.'

'I do not know you, *Monsieur*.'

'There is no need to worry,' said Charlie cheerfully. 'Here is a note from her.'

Paul took the note. It was certainly in Dédée's handwriting. Charlie followed him upstairs to the front room, where the grim interview of the evening before had taken place. Paul looked at the keen face of the young Frenchman.

'How is she? Where is she now?' he said anxiously.

'She has gone to Anglet. She wants to cross to Spain to see the British.'

'*Mon Dieu*, what will happen next!'

'She is anxious about Arnold Deppé.'

'I am afraid there is no doubt that he was arrested, and I have graver news. The Gestapo was here last night and questioned me and my family about Dédée for an hour. They have a full description of her.'

Charlie whistled.

'So, you see, *Monsieur*,' continued Paul. 'Dédée cannot come back to Belgium. She will certainly be caught if she does. You must persuade her to stay in France and work from there. I will take charge in Belgium.'

'When I return,' said Charlie, 'I will work for you.'

And Charlie, ready for action, soon said goodbye and walked again along the rainswept street. Within a week he had reached Anglet to warn Dédée of her peril.

When Charlie had gone, Paul put on his raincoat and hat and walked, as he did every morning, to the school in the Place Gauchard. It was a primary school for boys from seven to eleven among a maze of warehouses and grimy dwellings in a working-class district of Brussels. He stood for a moment in the playground and watched the boys playing merrily. Then he noticed a small boy, his hands clasped in misery, in a corner. Paul went across to him. The child moved as if to avoid him.

'What is it, Mario?'

At the sound of his kindly voice, Mario's tears flowed.

'He beat me,' he sobbed.

'Who?'

'My father.'

'Never mind, Mario. We have geography today. We shall learn all about the Congo.'

All that day, as he taught in the school and heard the laughter of the boys, Paul wondered what the future held for Dédée and those who worked with her.

How strange, he thought, that I should find myself a secret agent – *dans l'illégalité*. All my life I have been a man of peace, opposed to violence, imperialism and war. My tastes are simple. My favourite dish is herrings and potatoes.

He laughed a little to himself and went on with the lesson. Mario, catching the friendly glint of his spectacles in the sun, was smiling at his desk. If Paul could have foreseen where his admiration for youth and adventure would lead him!

Already he had begun to organise the collection of Allied servicemen and young Belgians in different parts of Belgium. He was constantly visiting patriots to seek their aid. Some offered him money; some were ready to shelter a man in their houses.

When the boys had gone home and the school was silent, Paul drew the blinds in his office, which adjoined the main hall. It had a door which led to an exit at the back of the building, a means of escape if the Gestapo came. There was a polite knock.

The young man who entered was Jean Ingels, known as Jean de Gand, and a stalwart helper of Paul from the earliest days of the Line. He had fine eyes with an earnest, remote expression. He sat before the schoolmaster's desk.

'I am going to make this office my headquarters for the present,' said Paul. 'We can meet here.'

'It is certainly safer than a private house.'

'What news?'

'I have been prospecting all over Flanders. I know of at least ten Englishmen hidden there,' said Jean Ingels.

Paul spoke vehemently:

'Everything depends on having a line to Spain. We must get some of them away. It is becoming too dangerous. People will not have confidence in us unless we get results!'

Suddenly there was the sound of someone crossing the hall. The two men fell silent, and Paul rose and peeped through the window in the office door.

'All right,' he said. 'It is Nadine.'

He opened the door.

A little, round-faced girl entered. She had a shy, artless expression.

Her name was Andrée Dumont. She looked no more than fifteen, though her true age was nineteen. Already her elfin figure was known in the Comet Line. She began her service with Comet by carrying messages for Paul in Brussels, but later she was one of his guides to Valenciennes and Paris. Paul, to avoid confusion with Dédée – another Andrée – called her Nadine.

Jean Ingels and Nadine were among Paul's first faithful companions. He was happy in their company and inspired by the vision of a great work of rescue.

He made his plans with Jean Ingels and Nadine for the dispatch of two soldiers of the ill-fated Highland Division, Bobby and Alan, to Spain.

'If Dédée must stay in France,' he said, 'we must have a new guide from Brussels to the French frontier.'

Then his thoughts went back to the slim, alert Frenchman, Charlie Morelle. He was the man.

The conference over, he shut his desk. Jean Ingels and Nadine said goodbye. Paul looked after them through the office window. When they were out of sight, he locked the main door of the school and hurried home along the dismal street.

## Chapter Four

# *En Route*

At the end of September, Tante Go arrived in Brussels from Anglet to collect the two men of the Highland Division, Bobby and Alan, from Paul. Her return journey with the Scotsmen to the Belgian frontier was uneventful, but at Quiévrain station there was a disturbing incident.

The two young Scotsmen had been told to represent themselves as Flemish. They had informed Tante Go that there was nothing in their pockets of interest to the Customs. But on arrival at Quiévrain, the presence of a German *Feldgendarme* made the French officials more alert than usual. To the horror of Tante Go, her companions were taken to an office and searched. Alan had a large quantity of cigarettes.

Both were told to wait while the *douanier* disappeared, leaving them in the office under the stolid gaze of the *Feldgendarme*. When his back was turned, Bobby began to stuff the cigarettes, taken from Alan, into his own pockets. The German, suddenly observing this, appeared highly amused and began to laugh. To Bobby's intense surprise he was allowed to leave with some of the cigarettes.

Alan waited dumbly in the office until the casual *Feldgendarme* disappeared. Through the open door, he saw Tante Go wave in the distance. He ran for all he was worth to join her. Then the three of them walked hastily away.

Suddenly there was a shout behind them. The *douanier* who had searched Alan was riding towards them on a bicycle, grinning broadly. He stopped and handed over to Alan the remainder of the cigarettes.

Then he said slyly to Tante Go:

'When you take birds like this about, don't wait for the Customs to empty their pockets. Do it beforehand. Good luck!'

From that day it was a strict rule of the Line that the pockets of escapers should be emptied before the journey. Anything incriminating, however valued and personal, must be left behind.

Bobby and Alan crossed the Pyrenees on 17 October, and Dédée, who accompanied them, was again in the Consul's office at Bilbao.

'Splendid,' he said, with real enthusiasm. 'But my superiors prefer that you should bring through airmen. They are more valuable to the war effort.'

Henceforward, the Consul was Dédée's firmest friend. His efforts on her behalf did much to establish the Line.

There began a hectic search for men of the Royal Air Force, shot down over Belgium. With Paul in charge at Brussels, Dédée set up her headquarters in Charlie's house at Valenciennes. From there she sent messages to her father.

'*Envoie-moi des enfants! Beaucoup d'enfants!*'

At this time raids over Belgium were few, and the survivors of crashed aircraft difficult to find. Often a farmer or an elderly couple, hiding an airman, refused to give him up until they trusted Paul and his friends. To inspire confidence, Dédée arranged with the British to broadcast messages on the BBC, to which all patriots listened every night.

'Wait until you hear "*La plume de ma Tante est noire*" just before the nine o'clock news. That will show you that we are genuine.'

Often these humdrum phrases gave encouragement and hope.

In the autumn of 1941 Charlie and his sister, Elvire Morelle, were the principal guides from Brussels to the Belgian frontier. Dédée took charge of the whole of the remaining journey to Bilbao.

Elvire Morelle was tall and strongly built. She did not much resemble her brother. She was robust, he was wiry. Her face was handsome, with steadfast brown eyes. While Charlie was lively and full of laughter, Elvire was quiet and restrained. She was to prove herself faithful to the Line in the midst of the worst perils.

In November 1941, she made her first journey as a guide from Brussels. It was one of those sad days of late autumn, when leaden clouds trail slowly across the sky and a light breeze flurries the leaves.

In Brussels, Paul had been active since dawn, collecting a party of two Polish and one Canadian airmen from their hiding places and bringing them, disguised and equipped with Belgian papers, to the Gare du Midi. Elvire, standing at the station entrance near groups of German soldiers on leave as they laughed and talked, waited for him. The clock struck seven. Paul's spare, slightly stooping figure appeared. He was followed in silence by three figures walking with un-Belgian gait. Their faces beneath their berets or caps were pale from long confine-ment indoors.

Paul took the tickets and, handing them to Elvire, bade the escapers farewell and disappeared among the crowds.

The airmen stared at Elvire in silent respect. They waited on the platform and then, boarding the train to Mons, sat in their compartment not daring to speak. There was an audible sigh from them as the express rattled over the points to the accompaniment of piercing whistles. The Canadian, unable to contain his excitement, wiped the sweat from his forehead with the back of his hand and grinned. An elderly man reading a newspaper glanced in his direction. Then the Canadian caught the sharp eyes of Elvire and subsided in his corner.

The train halted at Mons, and soon the fugitives were in the big station, watching the indicators. At a sign from their guide, they hurried along another platform to a country train, packed to the doors with workmen in blue overalls. As they sat on wooden seats, they listened to the rough chatter of the passengers. The train puffed slowly towards Quiévrain.

They reached the frontier station shortly after ten in the morning. The passengers moved in a stream to the Belgian Customs post. For the airmen it was a critical moment. The instructions of Elvire and Paul ran through their minds. They were pushed and jostled towards the *douaniers* holding before them pocketbooks with orange *Passierscheins* or frontier passes open in their hands. They remained close to the tall, comforting figure of Elvire as they passed the *douaniers* without incident. They had been told that if they were asked questions, they must let Elvire reply. Elvire, in her turn, was ready to explain that they were deaf and dumb!

The crowd surged down the platform to the French *douane* and, as they did so, Elvire caught a glimpse of the unobtrusive figure of Dédée standing among the waiting crowds at the far end of the platform. She was wearing a short brown coat over her dress. She showed no sign of recognition, but walked slowly towards the exit of the station, a little satchel on her back.

The French *douane* was passed. It had been a favourable day

for escapers and there had been a huge crowd crossing the frontier. Outside the station, two *Feldgendarmes*, in green uniform
with rifles, walked past them. The Germans took no notice of
ordinary passengers, but confined their attention to a few cars
and lorries at the control post.

The train for Valenciennes left Quiévrain with Dédée and
the three men seated together. They watched the homely figure
of Elvire as she waved goodbye. The journey was without incident and soon the party were in another train making for Douai
and Corbie, where they were to cross the Somme.

The airmen had now the chance to study their guide and
to observe each other. Weeks of waiting and hiding had made
them shy and silent. As the tension relaxed, they grinned at each
other, wondering where each had been shot down, what aircraft
he had been flying and from what station.

To the men, Dédée seemed reserved and shy. Her modest
looks intrigued them. She wore no make-up, nothing to attract
attention. When she laughed, it was at simple things, like the
jokes of an old café proprietor at Corbie, where they waited
until darkness before crossing the Somme. Often, she would
frown as if in deep thought.

In the cold November night, Dédée and the airmen silently
followed Pol, the tall guide, and François, the sixteen-year-old
grandson of an old man whose cottage stood on the riverbank.
Pol was dark and taciturn, but he, alone, knew the way through
the marshes. Cautiously, they followed him among the tangle of
reeds and willows. Whenever she saw the towpath bank loom-
ing ahead of her Dédée thought happily of Miss Richards and
the rubber tyre.

François waited beside a light skiff. There was the flutter

and splash of moorhens over the water. Listening, the fugitives could hear the distant whirr of a bicycle. Once more Dédée saw the sinister outline of a German helmet as the patrol passed.

They lay in the bushes waiting.

Pol whistled softly. From the other side of the river came an answering whistle. It was Nenette. Pol and François climbed on to the towpath, lifted the light craft and launched it. There was a muffled sound of rowlocks as Dédée heard the ripple of water against the far bank. The skiff went smoothly across. In five minutes they were making their way through soft, dewy fields to the farmhouse of Nenette. In her red-tiled kitchen they drank hot soup, then, exhausted, lay down to sleep on mattresses. It was past eleven, and the day had been long.

The Belgian papers, which the airmen had carried, were now of no value. They tore them up and threw them on the fire next morning, when Dédée took them by a country train to Amiens and thence to Paris.

In the early days of the Line the journey from Brussels to Bayonne was done without a halt in Paris. Dédée or Elvire booked a first-class compartment for the party. It was a wise precaution. Apart from the risk of controls, there was the need for the men to change into clothes suitable for the Spanish frontier region. Sometimes it was necessary to throw unwanted ties and hats out of the window. Later they were supplied with clothes in Paris.

The guides were in constant fear that the men would be interrogated and searched. Well-meaning passengers in waiting rooms would ask awkward questions. In such circumstances, the men were told to feign sleep or pretend to be deaf and dumb.

Sometimes these methods averted a crisis. At others, Dédée

or Elvire were obliged to create a diversion. On several occasions they threw their arms round their astonished charges and kissed them.

The party reached Paris, and by evening were at the Gare d'Austerlitz to take the train for the south. The crowds hurried to and fro in the fitful blackout of the station. There had been few air-raid alarms at this period of the war, but everywhere was a hushed expectancy. One day the Allies would come.

Dédée moved swiftly and silently through the shadowy groups of German and French travellers. She had a smooth grace as she wended her way untiringly to the train for Bayonne. The picture of her in the great station, where dangers loomed for her, was one of perfect dedication.

The men and the girl slept as the express to Bayonne carried them through the night. Sometimes two German military policemen, ignoring civilians, tramped down the corridor, examining leave passes. At dawn, the train raced through wild, flat country near Dax, then southwards till they saw the Bay of Biscay. The men watched from the windows as children wait for the first sight of the sea...

Dédée with the two Poles and the Canadian soon arrived at Bayonne. The men followed her along the platform. Their berets, though worn flat on their heads, as the Basques wore them, did not seem to suit them. Nor did they walk like young men of the region.

Dédée led them to the refreshment room of the station. In the crowd of travellers she caught sight of Janine's fair hair in the distance. Tante Go's daughter sat at a table with 'B' Johnson. Dédée bade the men sit down and spoke softly to Janine.

'All well?'

'Yes. I will take them straight to Urrugne. Tante Go wants to see you. Go to Anglet and join the men at the farm this evening.'

'B' Johnson whispered sepulchrally:

'The next move is Operation "Water Closet". To avoid having to pass the ticket barrier, each of you must follow one of us out of here to the station lavatories. There is a door there which leads out to the street. It unlocks on the inside and, as we have a duplicate of the key, it will be open.'

'B' grinned and walked from the refreshment room, followed by one of the Poles. When they reached the WC, 'B' pointed to a door.

'Go through there,' he said. 'Someone will be waiting for you outside.'

'B' returned to the refreshment room and unconcernedly ordered another cup of coffee.

The Pole gingerly opened the door and found himself in the forecourt of the station. Tante Go watched him emerge and motioned him to follow her to a small café.

The others followed. Dédée took the second Pole to the door and rejoined 'B' to leave the station a few minutes later by the main exit. The two airmen appeared from the lavatory door with Janine behind them.

Operation 'Water Closet' at Bayonne station was a great joke in the early days of the Line. Unluckily, another resistance group in the region had also acquired a key to the door and were arrested in the act of opening it.

Janine and the airmen bicycled to St Jean de Luz and, leaving their bicycles at the station, began to walk up the stony road to the farm at Urrugne. They marched at a sharp pace, and the exercise made Janine's cheeks glow. The men marvelled at her.

In the distance, a young Basque peasant on a bicycle was coming down the hill towards them. As he passed, he shook his head significantly and pointed up the road.

There was something wrong.

'Quick,' said Janine. 'Hide here.'

She pointed to a dip in the ground where they could lie concealed from the road.

'Stay here while I go forward and see what is happening.'

She scrambled up a wooded slope until she came to a clearing and saw once more the road which mounted to Urrugne. Only 100 yards away was a roadblock manned by German troops with bicycles. They were a frightening spectacle in the morning mist. Without hesitation, she returned to the airmen.

'Follow me.'

Her coolness gave them confidence, and they followed her on a long detour over bleak fields, strewn with boulders, until they were out of danger.

It was noon when they reached the farm at Urrugne. The door was opened by a tall man in a beret with a leather bottle in his hand.

'*Bonjour*, Florentino,' cried Janine.

## Chapter Five

# Florentino

After her first crossing to Bilbao in August 1941, Dédée, with the help of Tante Go, found a new guide in place of Thomas. His name was Florentino, a sturdy Basque. He lives today on the hill above Ciboure overlooking the bay of St Jean de Luz. In his little house decorations awarded him by four countries are displayed in frames. But Florentino is no longer able to guide secret travellers to Spain. One of his legs, shattered by German bullets, is shorter than the other. He limps over the rough roads and pines nostalgically for days gone by when, with Dédée at his side, he crossed the mountains in all weathers.

Each morning he goes to his work as a gardener in St Jean de Luz. As he comes down the steep hill to the quay of Ciboure, he passes the house of Madame Cataline Aguirre, Légion d'Honneur and Croix de Guerre. Cataline, the widow of a fisherman, hid many a fugitive before the last lap to Spain.

When Florentino returns at nightfall by the gaily coloured boats in the harbour, he passes a leafy dell where the escapers waited till all was clear before they set off for the hamlet of Urrugne. He can remember crouching behind the rough wall bordering the road and listening to the sound of jackboots in the southern night.

He can show the route by which his parties, avoiding the main road to Hendaye and Irun, climbed the ancient way to the farmhouse of Francia Usandizanga at Urrugne. What memories must that farmhouse hold for Dédée and Florentino! It was here that bronze-skinned Francia and her children prepared bowls of hot milk and soup for many a weary traveller. Here he dried his clothes, sodden with the mist and rain of the mountains. And upstairs was a clean bed where he slept until it was time to struggle on to Spain and freedom or return to the grim perils of Occupied France.

Francia's farmhouse has changed but little since the days of Comet. The rooms are sparsely furnished but newly swept, and from their windows is a glorious view of the mountains and, for more sinister purposes, a lookout over the stony road from St Jean de Luz. But the dark-eyed farmer's wife is gone. She paid for her devotion to Comet with her life.

In his prime Florentino was a tall man for a true Basque. His back was broad and his muscles splendid. He could carry a man on his shoulders across the racing torrent of the river Bidassoa. Like others of his countrymen, he had the quality of absolute loyalty to whatever cause he had chosen. Once decided on his course, nothing would shake him from it. Over him, too, the Cyclone cast her spell.

They were a strange pair: the great, powerful, illiterate man of the mountains, with his reverence for cognac and his indifference to fatigue and danger, and the quiet, tenacious Dédée. Together they shared the perils of twenty-five crossings of the Pyrenees with parties of men, returning safely together to the French side.

Florentino has a face of true grandeur. His features are at once fine and rugged, like a majestic animal. Standing in his garden on a summer's day among the bright flowers and butterflies of the region, he has an august beauty. His nose and mouth have the calm strength of one who communes with Nature. His hands are mighty. There is about his clothes a kind of nonchalance, and he wears his big flat beret balanced on his head.

He was delighted to work for Dédée and Tante Go. Like many of his fellow fBasques, he was a bitter enemy of Fascism. He ran serious risks. He was wanted by police on both sides of the frontier. The *carabineros* of France had been searching for him for months, and his activities had earned him the attention of the French *douane* and the Gestapo, by whom he was rightly suspected to be working for Allied intelligence.

Florentino's knowledge of the mountains was fabulous. He was able to find his way even when under the influence of copious quantities of cognac. He knew every path, every defile. He scented danger like a wild animal. His tremendous physical strength enabled him to withstand the rigours of constant journeys, summer and winter, from 1941 until the liberation of France in 1944.

If there was fog, damp and choking, blotting out every landmark, Florentino found the path. He would stop for a moment in his tracks, tapping the hard ground with his rope-soled shoes known as *espadrilles*. When he had found his way, he moved off at a great pace, with his party stumbling and slipping behind him. Often they called after him to go more slowly. He mumbled with impatience and came back and collected them.

Sometimes he stopped on the blackest night and marched to a tree trunk or a rock. He alone saw it in the gloom. He searched rapidly and brought forth a pair of *espadrilles* or a bottle of cognac left there months before.

He spoke only Basque. For the rest, '*doucement, doucement*', '*espere un poco*' and '*tais-toi*' were his foreign vocabulary.

The two Poles and the Canadian formed Dédée's third party to reach Spain in safety. On Christmas Eve 1941, with four British pilots, she made her fifth crossing since the formation of the Comet Line. As it grew dark she stood in the lamplight of Francia's kitchen, giving the last orders to the men. They were to march in single file and in complete silence until they were in the mountains. They must follow and obey their guide on the twenty-hour journey.

Florentino, in the orange glow of the lamp, sat packing a large rucksack. The light stressed the powerful lines of his face. He took a long swig at a bottle of cognac, then inspected each man, examining the fit of his *espadrilles*. Nothing could be more dangerous to the safety of the party than a man who lagged behind from blisters. He gave each a stout stick for the march.

It was a dark night, with a biting wind, which dropped suddenly as they walked in single file into the hills. Florentino carried the big rucksack on his back. Next, came Dédée with a pack containing her own small necessities: a skirt, a blouse and a pair of shoes. Finally, in obedient silence, came the airmen.

Thanks to the wind, the night was dry, and soon the stars began to show. The hills merged with the outline of the mountains, as the party found themselves looking towards a faint glow on the Spanish side. Behind them, the coast of France was impenetrable and full of foreboding.

They were halfway along the coast from St Jean de Luz when the strong beams of the lighthouse at Fuenterrabia swung across the hills, making grotesque shadows in the valleys. From the heights, they saw the twinkling lights of Spain. Below was

the frontier town of Irun at the mouth of the Bidassoa. Straining
their eyes, they could identify San Sebastián along the coast.

So far they had been climbing upwards. Now began the
descent into the valley of the Bidassoa. The weather had changed
once more and a fine snow began to fall. The path grew slippery,
and despite their sticks, the airmen, unpractised in climbing,
often fell heavily. Bruised and shaken, they picked themselves
up and scrambled on among the rocks, clinging to the roots of
trees and shrubs.

One after another, the kindly lights of neutral territory
disappeared as the party sank into the shadow of the river gorge.
Fortunately, the night had been dry save for a brief snowstorm.
Had there been heavy rain, it would have made the Bidassoa
impassable on foot. That would have meant a long detour and
the crossing of a bridge lit by floodlights. The route was five
hours longer and there would have been grave risk of capture
by the Spaniards.

Suddenly they could see the faint grey gleam of the roadway
which runs on the Spanish bank of the river. From time to time
a car passed along the frontier road, its headlamps briefly illu-
minating the torrent of the Bidassoa in the valley. Parallel with
the road there was a railway on a step of sheer rock. In the far
distance, was the red glow of an engine.

The descent proceeded painfully in the cold air of Christmas
night. The sweet sound of church bells was borne on the wind.
It comforted the party as they struggled down.

At first there was only a smooth, regular noise, like that of a
giant motor. Then it became more distinct. It was the deep roar
of the torrent bounding towards the sea at Irun. They could
see white, luminous foam dancing before them in the darkness

and, looking through branches of trees, saw below them the Bidassoa, tumbling and twisting between the rocks.

Florentino held up his hand for silence and peered across the river. Not far from their hiding place was a brightly lit frontier post. There were figures of men walking beside it. It was known that frontier guards patrolled the road. They would not hesitate to fire if they saw anyone trying to cross.

Florentino removed his trousers and tied them in a bundle. Dédée, wearing blue fisherman's trousers, took them off and knotted them round her neck, telling the men to do the same. It was dangerous to make any noise or show movement.

Florentino climbed carefully down into the turbulent water. He tested the depth. The river was fordable. Then, holding the hand of the first escaper, he led him across, with the water up to his waist. It was safe enough. When the stream was high, one false slip into deep water meant death. Dédée, too, forged into the river. She had crossed it several times before. Confidently, she took one of the airmen by the hand and helped him over. She was strong and vital. No one thought of her as a woman. She was the chief.

They rested in a sodden meadow before climbing a rocky embankment to reach the railway line. Shivering from the icy water, they put on their trousers and tried to restore their circulation. Their feet dragged wearily in the swampy ground.

The sternest test was yet to come. With Florentino in front, they climbed on to the railway and, clinging to the thick bushes growing above it, dragged themselves level with the road. This was the moment of the greatest danger: the crossing of the road into Spain, followed by the ascent of a steep slope on the far side.

Florentino lay flat, hidden by a thorn bush, watching the road. He pushed aside the branches and observed the frontier post. There was light enough from its windows for him to see a sentry patrolling 100 yards away. He gave a kind of grunt, jumped quickly on to the road, then noiselessly ran across and scrambled up the slope opposite. Pulling himself upwards with the help of roots and bushes, his great strength enabled him to get clear of the road and out of sight in a matter of seconds. The weary escapers lumbered after him. One fell back into the road with a clatter. Dédée, who had waited to see that all were safely across, seized him under the arm and pushed him up the bank. She possessed a vigour and courage which vied with those of Florentino himself.

The crossing of the frontier on that Christmas night was without mishap, but there were nights when Dédée and Florentino escaped by a hair's breadth. One night in July 1942, they were ambushed on the French side by two German soldiers. The party of airmen were scattered till Dédée, coolly collecting them, took them back to Urrugne, whence they crossed safely two days later.

Sometimes a man lost touch with the party in the darkness and found himself alone in dangerous territory with the threat of the Spanish concentration camp at Miranda before him. But few lost their way. Before the start at Urrugne, Dédée and Florentino always indicated on the map their landmarks: the lighthouse of Fuenterrabia, and the lights of Irun; the Bidassoa; the peaks of the Trois Couronnes.

The climb was arduous. The escapers were beginning to tire after their long march. It seemed that the journey uphill would never end. Far ahead, despite his heavy rucksack, Florentino climbed steadily in the crisp mountain air. His head cleared quickly from the effects of cognac or the contents of his *bota*, a goatskin bottle filled with native wine. The farther he marched, the more powerful his strides became.

'*Dos cien metros*,' he said laughingly, to indicate that the resting place was near.

The panting fugitives struggled a few yards farther upwards. But with Florentino it was always '*dos cien metros*'. He did not concern himself with measurements. He lived by signs. He knew the feel of the path. He could find each goat track in the darkness. He could recognise some obscure landmark momentarily revealed by a parting in the mist.

Dédée alone kept pace with him. The men behind could see her slim but powerful legs as she followed the guide up the mountain.

At the top of the slope the party lay down. When they had got their breath, they smoked and ate bread and cheese. Florentino refreshed himself from his *bota*, then offered it round. It warmed the tired climbers, but Dédée firmly restrained them from drinking more than a measure. There were several hours of marching yet. Save for the whistling of the wind in the crannies, there was no sound. They could now see once more the faint glow of the lights of Spain like a halo in the sky before them.

The march was resumed. The ground beneath their feet was more even, but the men felt that they could go no farther. Dédée, her small, determined figure faintly outlined, cheered them on. Her mild taunts and quiet commands made them ashamed of their weariness. How could they fail before this extraordinary girl? The force of her example drove them on through the night. Sometimes she turned to one who lagged behind and spoke soothingly, giving him the will to continue.

At last they neared the end of the crossing. Florentino cautiously followed the road which circles below the trio of peaks of the Trois Couronnes. The way began to mount once more. They must hurry on, for the dawn was beginning to show. The men, sweating and exhausted, their clothes soaked with dew, began to lag behind again. Dédée sharply reproved them. In a few minutes she pointed to a splendid panorama of lights stretching into the far distance. They were on the other side of the mountain, and Spain lay before them.

As dawn broke they were among fresh fields and the tinkling of sheep-bells. They moved down into a valley, and soon in the grey light the roof of a farmhouse, showed above the mist. They approached it carefully, watching for the green uniforms and cocked hats of *carabineros*.

Florentino flung a pebble at the window, and the door was opened by a robust Spanish woman, who bustled about her kitchen aiding everyone to dry their clothes. She made them a wonderful omelette or *tortilla*, so that the escapers, well fed and happy, soon fell asleep.

While the men slept, Dédée changed into the blouse and skirt she had brought with her, and, walking across the fields for five kilometres, came to the town of Renteria. She took the tram to San Sebastián and went to the flat of her friend, Bernardo, where she rested until it was dark. Then, with Bernardo driving his car, she returned to the farmhouse to collect the men. Bernardo drove back with them along the main road to San Sebastián. He stopped suddenly at the sight of a stationary car.

'Here we are,' said Dédée.

The bewildered airmen stepped out into the darkness. Then they noticed the CD plates on the car. They were bustled inside to be taken to the British Consulate. They had only a moment to shake hands with Dédée and Bernardo before they were driven away.

There was no time to wait. Dédée must rejoin Florentino and be back in the mountains before dawn broke. As Bernardo drove back to the farm, Dédée thought in triumph that her plan to take men direct to the British and save them from a Spanish concentration camp was succeeding.

In February 1942, Elvire Morelle joined Dédée and Florentino in the passage of the Pyrenees. It was her first crossing. Elvire, big and strongly built, found the way harder than Dédée, who was light and nimble and used to climbing.

They made the crossing to San Sebastián without mishap, with a lone Englishman and Florentino, and on 6 February began the return journey with their guide in driving snow. The two girls, following him, could see little in the blizzard. There was a sharp cry of pain. Elvire had fallen with her leg doubled beneath her. Dédée examined the leg in the light of a torch. It was badly fractured.

Florentino, quick to appreciate the danger, for it was getting light, went off in search of a mule from one of the mountain farms.

The two girls were alone in a hostile land, unsheltered from the icy wind. At dawn came fine rain, soaking them to the skin. Elvire was in great pain, her head resting against a lichen-covered rock. Dédée, searching, found two flat pieces of wood and improvised a splint.

Florentino returned with the mule, and Elvire, with much difficulty, was mounted on it and led to an empty hut. She awaited darkness in great agony on a bed of ferns. As night fell again, she began once more her tortured ride down slippery ways to the farmhouse near Renteria, whence she had set out the evening before. Next day, Bernardo arrived from San Sebastián and drove her to his flat, and there a Basque doctor operated on the leg. The fracture had been untended for forty-eight hours, but, thanks to his skill, Elvire recovered.

Dédée and Florentino could not ignore the terrible dangers of this incident, but they did not foresee that it was the beginning of a series of tragedies for the Line. In Brussels the sands were running out for Paul.

In February the Secret Police of the Luftwaffe called at No. 73. Paul was in Valenciennes, but Suzanne had an unpleasant hour of interrogation in the front room. The subject again was Dédée and her whereabouts.

The police said nothing of Paul at this interview, but next day a woman neighbour of Madame De Jongh reported that they had questioned her about him.

Paul must act quickly. He changed his headquarters to the house of two old ladies at Uccle. He was just in time. Six weeks later, ten Luftwaffe policemen burst into his home and arrested Madame De Jongh and Suzanne. They were released the same day, but it had been a near thing.

Paul did not cease his restless activity. He obtained leave of absence from his post as head master. To disguise himself, he grew side whiskers. The price on his head was a million Belgian francs.

At last his friends persuaded him to flee to Paris and he left Brussels for ever on 30 April. Six days later, Charlie Morelle and Henri Micheli, to whom Paul had entrusted his command, were arrested in Brussels as they sat at dinner.

The arrest of Charlie Morelle was a tragic blow. He had been a splendid inspiration, this daring Frenchman, to those who worked with him. From the day when Madame Maréchal of the Avenue Voltaire had sheltered him, and Dédée had helped him to escape, he had been a fine exponent of the risky task of guide. His loss was a personal tragedy to his friends. His capture was another grim landmark in the history of the Comet Line. It was the end of the pioneer group formed by Paul and Dédée in Belgium.

Out of the bitter days of confusion of May 1942, there appeared a new genius, a great chief: the Baron Jean Greindl, alias Nemo.

## Chapter Six

# Nemo

In 1942, Jean Greindl was living in his father's house at Zellick near Brussels. The house, a square, white country mansion, is approached by a lane which gently descends from the paved main road to Ghent.

Zellick is a cluster of dull brick and mauve-brown roofs on either side of the tramway to the capital. It was once beloved by the painter, Breughel. Here he painted 'La Kermesse' amid the apple orchards and surrounding hills.

A new road named

Baron Jean Greindl Laan
11th September, 1943

leads out of the principal street.

Jean Greindl was thirty-six when he first encountered the Comet Line. He had heard from friends of the work of Paul and Dédée and he longed to help them.

Like Paul and many others, Jean Greindl was overwhelmed by the *débâcle* of 1940. At first he sought in vain to find a way of helping the Allies. Then, in the early part of 1942, he became director of a canteen run by the Swedish Red Cross in Brussels. This institution, famous in the annals of the Comet Line, was known as the *Cantine Suédoise*. Its headquarters were in the Rue Ducale. Through its *patron*, a Swedish lady, Madame Scherlinck, it provided food and clothes for the poor and ailing children of the city.

Jean Greindl was surrounded by voluntary helpers, and a rosy-faced commandant, Bidoul, kept the accounts. His head-quarters in the Rue Ducale were in a half-furnished house of early nineteenth-century Brussels. His office was a long, half-panelled room, which had perhaps been the library of the house. The furniture was old and the carpets worn. Everywhere there was dust and decay. The windows looked on to a desolate garden.

The *Cantine* itself, where the children fed, had a makeshift air. It was in the basement beneath the office, a bare room with tables and forms. Leading from it was a dark, old-fashioned kitchen. From this frugal place Jean Greindl could hear in his office above the clatter of plates and the sound of eager young voices.

He was pleased with this work, for he was efficient and humane. His family had played a famous part in the develop-ment of the Belgian Congo, and much of his life had been spent in the management of a coffee plantation.

At first the atmosphere of the drab old house was strange to him after the action of his early life. For he was accustomed to command. He had a singular force of character and kindliness.

To his friends in Belgium he was 'Le Kas', an affection-ate shortening of the title given him by native workers in the Congo. As he became concerned with the work of resistance, he dropped his name and was called 'Nemo'. Some said it was after the romantic commander of the *Nautilus* in Jules Verne's *20,000 Leagues under the Sea*.

Each morning Nemo walked down the lane from the mansion of Zellick to take the tram to the *Cantine Suédoise*. His face was lean and strong, his ears rather prominent. His firm nose and mouth suggested vigour and resolve. He had fine, humorous, grey-blue eyes. His long, sensitive hands suggested a sharp intellect.

Punctually at nine-thirty each morning, the staff of the *Cantine Suédoise* greeted his immaculate figure. Despite its voluntary nature, Nemo ran the *Cantine* as if it were a coffee plantation. On his arrival, papers were placed on his desk in the dingy office. He would then confer with benevolent, rotund Commandant Bidoul, who acted as Registrar. Gravely, they would discuss supplies of flour, potatoes and powdered egg and, sometimes, the menus for the children's meals. Often Madame Scherlinck, the Swedish benefactress of the poor, visited the office. Eccentric and kindly, she would appear without warning, dressed in riding breeches, and tapping her boots with a smart crop as she asked questions of Nemo and Commandant Bidoul. Nemo would be brief, efficient and courteous. He would escort her to the door and then descend to the basement, where he mingled with the children in his gruff and kindly way.

His contacts with Paul and Dédée had been slight. In 1941, Nemo had met a girl with splendid, bronze-red hair, who lived at Hal, near Brussels. Her name was Peggy van Lier. Nemo was immediately impressed by her. At that time, he was anxiously seeking to foster resistance to the Germans, and in Peggy he found a useful ally. She was serious and brave, and they became firm friends. They wrote secret notes to each other as part of their plans to help young Belgians to escape to England.

Peggy had come to know Jean Ingels, known as Jean de

Gand, Paul's second in command, and Dédée herself. In this haphazard way, Peggy and Nemo became acquainted with Dédée and Paul.

From the early part of 1942, Nemo had delivered bags of rice and flour from the stores of the Swedish Red Cross to Paul. These were distributed among the families which sheltered airmen.

He became more and more involved in the Line. The bills for the children's food disappeared from his desk early in the morning. Instead, there appeared mysterious pieces of coloured cardboard, blank forms and certificates and rubber stamps. Sometimes they would be hurriedly crushed into a drawer on the arrival of the eccentric Madame Scherlinck.

When Paul had left for Paris, the storm clouds still gathered over his intrepid family. Suzanne, after her father's departure, worked courageously in the face of growing danger. With Nemo, she took up the threads of her father's scattered team. For her, the work involved the greatest risk.

It was Peggy van Lier, with her red hair worn in careless fashion, who became his right hand. Like others who later formed part of Nemo's operational staff, she came to help with the feeding of the children. This voluntary organisation provided a cover for secret work for several young people. Nemo became their leader. He was, in a sense, the counterpart of the brilliant, enchanting Dédée. Both of them have an assured place among those whose lives will remain a shining example of faith and courage.

Every morning Peggy came to the office where Nemo was sitting at his desk. She was lightly built and moved like Dédée, as though she possessed some more-than-ordinary energy. Her companions thought of her as always running.

As she entered the room, Nemo stood up. He gave her a welcoming smile, shook her hand firmly and said, '*Quoi de neuf?*'

His eyes twinkled as if the task of rescuing airmen from the enemy was a huge joke.

Peggy sat on the arm of the chair, smoking. Nemo quietly gave orders.

'Peggy,' he said, 'I shall have a job for you tomorrow. I am expecting some more parcels.'

'Hooray!'

Peggy jumped from her chair and began to skip about the room. Nemo, watching her benignly, wondered if she understood. She and her young friends, unmarked by the cares of middle age, thought of their work as a thrilling pastime. It was for them a golden period of life. There was an aura of romance about their abrupt, sardonic leader. To the boys and girls who worked for him, he would say:

'*Toujours l'audace!*'

There was the sound of laughter outside the office and, without ceremony, two young men rushed into the room. There was Georges d'Oultremont, fresh-faced and laughing, who replaced Andrée Dumont, known as Nadine, the brave little girl who had worked for Paul. Since the spring, she and her family had been in the grim prison of St Gilles in Brussels. The other was his cousin, Edouard, tall, handsome and fair-haired; a military figure. Like Georges, he became a guide from Brussels to Paris.

They were a remarkable group, these first helpers of Nemo. Peggy, alert and happy, still sat on the arm of the chair. Georges, in plus fours, sat on a table in the centre of the room, swinging his legs.

Nemo announced his plans for rebuilding the Line. He proposed to divide Belgium into regions for the collection of survivors of crashed aircraft. He had already arranged 'reporting centres' at Gand, Namur, Liège and Hasselt. To these centres, patriots in surrounding villages and farms were to bring news of '*les enfants*'.

Nemo gave his orders for the week.

'Peggy!' She stood to attention. 'Go to Xavier, the printer, and get some more identity cards by tomorrow...'

'Georges!' He slipped from the table on which he had been sitting. 'Can you swim?'

'No,' replied Georges. 'But this is only Monday – by Thursday I shall have learned.'

There was laughter. Then Nemo spoke seriously.

'I have heard rumours that the control of the Somme, which was relaxed last year, may be reimposed. It might mean that we can no longer take the men direct by rail to Paris. We must prepare for them to be taken across the river again... Peggy! What are you looking at?'

All eyes were turned towards the window. A large German staff car stood at the entrance to the house. Spellbound, they watched an orderly jump out and open the door. Nemo quickly seized a small piece of paper with a secret address from Peggy and stuffed it into the finger of his glove. There was a glimpse of field-grey and scarlet outside. A trim, military figure in General's uniform left the car and came to the door.

'*Mon Dieu!*' said someone. 'It is von Falkenhausen!' Generaloberst von Falkenhausen was Commander-in-Chief in Belgium and northern France. Whatever could he be doing at the *Cantine*? Nemo was unruffled:

'All of you run down to the dining room. I will deal with this.'

He felt anxious, but inquisitive, as he went into the hall. The General was standing there with a staff officer. He was thin, monocled and aristocratic. He spoke politely to Nemo:

'Are you the manager?'

'Yes.'

'I wanted to see my friend, Madame Scherlinck. Is she here?'

Nemo detected a faint embarrassment in the cold, grey eyes of the General.

'No, I am afraid not.'

The General bowed swiftly, saluted and was gone. Nemo could scarcely restrain his laughter and relief. As he returned to his office, his eye caught a banner displayed in the hall carrying a message in Swedish:

'In Memory of Queen Astrid. Help the Children of Belgium.'

Nemo reflected that the correct von Falkenhausen would have been deeply disturbed to know of the 'children' whom Madame Scherlinck's Swedish Cantine now served.

During the summer of 1942, Nemo and his team worked hard to build up the Line. His organisation grew and flourished. As more planes crashed on Belgian territory the work increased and, with the devoted help of Peggy, Georges, Edouard and Jean Ingels, the men were taken to Paris, where Paul, after his flight from his home, had established his own collecting point for 'parcels'.

These were the loyal assistants of Nemo in his task of reconstruction. Every morning they would crowd his office, to the deep concern of poor Commandant Bidoul, who sighed as he sat at his desk:

'*Ça finira mal, Monsieur le Baron! Ça finira mal!*'

In July, the Line was functioning smoothly again and Dédée could announce to the British that, for the moment, the damage had been repaired.

Nemo had never met her. He had heard tales of her prowess. She had fast become a legend from Brussels to the Spanish frontier.

One morning, he received a mysterious summons to the house of a friend in Brussels. He went there, anxious lest it be a trap.

When he arrived, his faithful colleague, Suzanne, her homely face smiling happily, was there.

'What is all this about?'

'Wait and see. I have a surprise for you.'

And she opened the door. A girl was standing by the window, wearing a short, flowered dress. Nemo knew instantly, though he had never seen her, that it was Dédée.

Suzanne had met her sister Dédée only a few minutes before. The two girls had been overjoyed to see each other again. There was a moment of tears and congratulation. Dédée was brimful of enthusiasm for her work. Despite the fatigue of continual long journeys, she was a picture of courage and determination. At this moment she was excited and voluble.

'What is being done for Charlie? We must try to save him!'

'We are doing all we can,' said Nemo. 'You must have patience, Dédée. We are in touch with a lawyer known as "Y". He knows a German officer who has influence with the Gestapo.'

'How much do they want?'

Dédée paced the room thoughtfully. Nemo looked at her, smiling gravely.

'We shall need 300,000 francs at least.'

'How are we going to get it?'

'I am in contact with those who can supply the money. Our friend "Y" is a lawyer. He is a careful man. He thinks the German is safe.'

Dédée looked at him impatiently and walked towards the window. Then she turned and said vehemently:

'But meanwhile Charlie is being beaten and tortured.'

Nemo shrugged his shoulders.

'I am doing all I can.'

He turned the conversation to the future of the Line. He described to Dédée how he had begun with Jean Ingels and Suzanne Wittek. Dédée spoke seriously as the time came for him to leave:

'You have really thrown in your lot?'

'Yes, of course.'

Nemo was amused at her earnestness. She frowned. Then she said something he was to remember many times:

'You realise that there are nine chances out of ten that you will not come out of this alive?'

Nemo was still smiling. He shrugged his shoulders once again in a slight gesture of acceptance. They shook hands. They were to meet but three times more.

## Chapter Seven

# Rue Oudinot

In May 1942, Dédée and her father, Paul, were reunited in Paris. They had not seen each other since January of that year, when Dédée had paid a daring visit to her home in Brussels.

After several months of absence, she was overcome by homesickness. She appeared suddenly one snowy evening at the door. Her family were overjoyed.

Next day, after a happy lunch party, they talked together in the front room. Beside the window overlooking the street was Martin Wittek, the twelve-year-old stepson of Suzanne. He was watching for any sign of danger. Suddenly he cried:

'Quick, the Gestapo!'

'Don't be silly, Martin.'

'Then come and look.'

Dédée glanced into the street.

A car had stopped outside No. 73 Avenue Émile Verhaeren. Two officers of the Secret Field Police were leaving it. Dédée rushed to the kitchen, where her wellington boots and mackintosh were ready for emergency. Without a word, she opened the French windows and dashed down the pathway of the garden at the back of the house, followed by Frédéric, Martin's elder brother. She reached the wall at the end and, with his assistance, leapt over it. Running across some wasteland, she came to a street on the far side of the Avenue Émile Verhaeren and hid in a friend's house.

Sixteen-year-old Frédéric calmly smudged out her footprints in the snow on the lawn as the Gestapo again demanded of Paul:

'Where is Andrée De Jongh?'

Undaunted by the tragic arrest of Charlie Morelle, Paul determined to start work again in Paris.

The Rue de Babylone, on the south bank of the Seine, is a street of sad, grey houses of the Second Empire. A gloomy *maison de repos* for priests overshadows the apartment houses on the other side. Each house has an archway leading to a small paved court overgrown with weeds. The paint has faded and cracked on the woodwork of the windows. It was in this street that Paul found faithful friends.

Not far from the junction of the Rue Vaneau and the Rue Oudinot is No. 37 Rue de Babylone. There are polished, winding stairs to the fourth-floor flat, where lives a handsome, grey-haired lady. She is Germaine, widow of Robert Aylé.

The flat is crowded with small, exquisite furniture.

There are cabinets of china and finely bound books. Germaine has taste and dignity which has followed much suffering. She sits there serenely with her memories, though she has seen terrible things. She alone of the little group which gathered in her discreet sitting room ten years before survived the violent days of Comet.

Robert Aylé was forty-five when he first encountered Paul and Dédée in the summer of 1942. He was typically French. He had dark brown hair brushed back from a fine, high forehead. His face was compelling and genial. His eyes were what the French call *noisette*.

Robert was mercurial and humorous. Paul was mild and scholarly, but never was there a firmer alliance between Belgium and France.

Robert had worked for the resistance movement in France for a long time before his meeting with Paul. With his fierce hatred of the Germans, the rescue of Allied pilots and airmen seemed a mission worthy of any risk. His first act was to help the Comet organisation to find a suitable headquarters in Paris.

Paul and Dédée required an *appartement* where they could stay unmolested and, if necessary, conceal some of their charges. Elvire Morelle, who had joined forces with them, rented a huge, ugly villa at St Maur, on the outskirts of Paris, during the summer months of 1942. There the men could stay in comfort and bask in the sun behind the high garden wall. Elvire was housekeeper and cook and Charlie, her brother, would often appear at the house, bringing a new group of airmen from Brussels.

The two elderly ladies who owned the house had earnestly demanded of their tenants that care should be taken of the hideous stained-glass windows on the staircase.

'You see, *Monsieur*, they are precious. We inherited them from our grandmother!'

'Please do not worry, *mesdames*,' said Charlie. 'Except when I am here, there will only be ladies in the house.'

The windows often narrowly escaped damage when high-spirited games were played on the stairs. One hot afternoon the kindly old ladies suddenly appeared at the gate. They were a little short-sighted, or they would have seen the latest fugitives, clad only in towels, vanishing into the house. Elvire, her leg still in plaster after her accident in the Pyrenees, hobbled towards them. She was anxious that they should not see five men's shirts drying on the line, and so diverted them to another part of the garden. They tenderly enquired after her health. There was great hilarity after this incident, but there was also no more sunbathing on the lawn, in case the *mesdames* appeared again to enquire after Elvire's health.

The villa at St Maur, for all its comfort and seclusion, was too far from the main stations of Paris. It involved risky journeys to the quiet suburb, where strangers were noticed. Elvire therefore acquired the lease of a flat, in her own name, in a street which adjoined the Rue de Babylone, a few doors from Robert Aylé. It was on the fourth floor of a block of modern *appartements*, at No. 10, Rue Oudinot.

On the fifth floor above Elvire's flat lived a courageous Norman, Aimable Fouquerel. He worked as a *masseur* at a hospital nearby, which necessitated frequent absences at night. This capable, generous and loyal man put his flat at the disposal of the organisation. Sometimes, when there were many airmen waiting to be sent on to the frontier, three of them would sleep on his large bed. To this day, the flat is much as it must have been when Aimable, with his unassuming smile, would go off to his work, leaving the fugitives to while away the time before leaving for Spain. At the back of the building there are the barracks of the *Gardes Republicaines* – a block of sour, grey buildings. Dédée and her father, studying it from Elvire's flat, would laugh together as they discussed what to do if the Gestapo called. Paul declared that he would pull a chest of drawers against the door while Dédée tore sheets and made a rope for them to descend to the courtyard of the barracks.

Paul, Robert and Aimable formed a small, unobtrusive group, moving cautiously through the dim streets. Elvire, as robust and inscrutable as ever, would superintend the feeding and clothing of the men, aided by an indomitable Madame Laurentie, who lived on the second floor. For nearly a year airmen and soldiers were hidden in these three small flats, and not a soul in the building, save the old concierge, knew the truth.

After the tragedies of the past few weeks, when their grief at the first major catastrophe of the Line had begun to wane, Paul and his friends felt themselves once more secure. It seemed to them that for the present the worst was over. Nemo was superbly successful, and soon there came a tremendous outburst of activity. In the months of July, August, September and October, 1942, thirteen parties were sent down to Tante Go at Anglet. Dédée and Florentino personally conducted fifty-four men over the Pyrenees.

But in July the ill-fated attempt of the lawyer known as 'Y' to intervene with the Germans to save Charlie Morelle brought disaster. The 300,000 francs provided for the German intermediary were quickly seized by the Gestapo. Their inquiries into the whole rash transaction led them to Suzanne and her arrest in July. For her the remainder of the war became a series of cruel months in solitary confinement at the prison of St Gilles and, later, at Mauthausen and Ravensbrück.

During 1942 and 1943, blow after blow struck the gallant family De Jongh. Already, at the time of Suzanne's arrest, they were scattered. Suzanne's husband was an Austrian, and he had already reached England. Her stepson, Frédéric, whose *sang-froid* had helped Dédée to escape from her home in the snow, followed his father some months afterwards. And in the autumn came the turn of Madame De Jongh and frail old Tante Nini. The Gestapo, on one of their searches for Paul and Dédée, hustled them off to a cellar beneath their headquarters. They had searched the house clumsily while a large, uncouth soldier stood guard over Madame De Jongh as she superintended the boiler that supplied her central heating with philosophic calm. After much blustering by the Germans, the two elderly ladies were released the same day. They were to meet the Gestapo many times more and to be imprisoned in St Giles as hostages in 1943.

As he sat in the flat at the Rue Oudinot, straining his short-sighted eyes to fill in false papers for the airmen, Paul's anxiety for Dédée grew. In the autumn of 1942, the Cyclone had already crossed the mountains a score of times in both directions. The journey was sufficient to exhaust an average man who had only the pleasant anticipation of reaching neutral territory to occupy his thoughts. Dédée had to make the long journey back on each occasion. She had to run the gauntlet of *gendarmes*, *douaniers* and *Feldpolizei* on her exhausting journeys from Paris. Always in her mind was her fear for Paul and her family. One night, returning from Spain, she and Florentino were ambushed by *carabineros*. In her flight, she fell and cut her legs. The wounds became septic, and when she returned to Paris she was feverish. The doctor who saw her was an unconscious humorist.

'You need some rest, young lady. You need a holiday in the mountains!'

The wounds healed, but the dangers grew. It was not only the *carabineros* who must be avoided: the French *gendarmes* of the district of St Jean de Luz, patrolling at dawn at the approaches to the frontier, once came upon her as she trudged down the hill

from Urrugne after another tiring journey from Bilbao. It was
five o'clock in the morning, and there was a high wind. Dédée
was very weary. Shadows appeared suddenly before her.

'*Halte!*'

It was no use running. It must be brazened out.

The *gendarmes* took her papers, her *certificat de domicil.*

'You do not come from this district, *Mademoiselle.*'

'Oh, yes. I am living here with my aunt in Anglet.'

'You do not look like a native of these parts.'

Her papers were in order. They let her go, but the incident
must be a warning. It was not enough to dye one's hair jet black
and pretend to be half a Spaniard.

But her exacting life had its lighter moments, even in the
presence of danger. There was the British Army officer who,
questioned by a *Feldgendarme*, had escaped by pretending to
be a mental defective. Or the moment when an airman in a
crowded train, which had stopped for a short time at a signal on
the way to Bayonne, was asked by some bustling paterfamilias:

'Is this St Pierre des Corps, *Monsieur?*'

The airman had only one word of French.

'*Oui.*'

The door was flung open on a pitch-dark, rainy night. The
family stepped down on to the line, pulling their luggage after
them as the train began to move away. They were fifteen kilometres from St Pierre des Corps.

Dédée recalls, even today, many of these 'incidents'. Outside
the Gare d'Austerlitz there was a hoarding on which a poster
still advertised the night train to London, a mute remembrance
of past holidays:

'Good evening, Paris. Good morning, London.'

She would often pass this poster, and the little group of airmen, with their guide, would laugh silently.

But Dédée knew that as the numbers of airmen to be rescued grew, she could not carry on the Line from Paris to Bilbao alone. Very soon afterwards the inhabitants of the Rue Oudinot noticed Paul with a new companion. He was a Belgian, though pale and Latin in appearance. His hair was dark and his face well moulded, with high cheekbones. He had an air of great faith and conviction. He was Jean-François Nothomb, alias Franco. His strange nickname derived from Franquito, which Elvire had called him affectionately.

Franco had been introduced to Nemo in Brussels by Georges d'Oultremont, and Nemo, in response to requests from Paris for an aide to Dédée, sent him to join her and her father at the Rue Oudinot. As soon as Dédée saw him, she made him her lieutenant.

The companions of the Rue Oudinot, harassed by their long exertions, were delighted with him. In the fourth-floor flat the table would be cleared and Franco and Elvire would wash the dishes in the kitchen while Paul and Dédée would settle down to their nightly task: the filling in of identity cards and the forging of signatures. They would also fix passport photographs, taken by a little photographer in a small shop in the Boulevard Raspail. Studying these photographs, they found much cause for amusement.

'Tom makes a good priest!'

'Yes,' replied Elvire. 'He was rather confused today, poor fellow. As he was walking down the Rue de Babylone, a whole group of priests came past. He did not realise that he ought to have bowed to them as they passed. They very nearly came up and spoke to him.'

Tom was just another escaping airman, trusting in the skill of Dédée and her friends. He sat upstairs in the flat of Aimable, the masseur, with two fellow escapers. There they read and smoked and exchanged reminiscences. They felt they were in the hands of some Scarlet Pimpernel organisation.

With the arrival of Franco, the escape line acquired a new life. He was soon acting as a guide from Paris to Anglet, where he made the acquaintance of Tante Go. From there he did his first trip over the mountains, and it was unforgettable. That first view of the lights of San Sebastián far below! It was heartening to escape from the monotony of occupation.

Franco was destined to play a great and heroic part in the history of the Line and he was to be fortified in his task by a deep religious faith. In that moment, as he looked down on the lights of San Sebastián, Franco could not know how soon his testing time would come.

After the splendid successes of the summer, the number of raids diminished and the comrades of the Rue Oudinot and the *Cantine Suédoise* grew restless.

Then, without warning, came the second disastrous blow to the Comet Line.

## Chapter Eight

# Avenue Voltaire

In the autumn, a little, dark girl joined the group at the *Cantine*. Her name was Elsie Maréchal, the daughter of the same Madame Maréchal, the Englishwoman who had hidden Charlie Morelle and many other fugitives from the Germans. Elsie was a friend of Dédée, whom she regarded with the deepest admiration. Despite the anxiety of her parents, she became a trusted messenger of Nemo. She spoke English perfectly. Her task was to cross-examine airmen collected from the provinces. Her innocent questions, asked with schoolgirl charm, tested their stories. Over all hung the fear of a traitor, who might penetrate the Line as a cancer grows in the body.

In those days all Belgian guides brought their charges to the Square Frère Orban in Brussels. And there, on the steps of St Joseph's Church, they would be handed over to Elsie.

The password was:

'What's the time?'

'Always the same.'

Then Elsie would put questions to the airmen on the steps of the church about their service and the aeroplanes they flew. When she had made up her mind they were genuine, she took them inside the church. These were Nemo's orders. Elsie would leave them in a pew while she hastened to the *Cantine Suédoise* to report.

Messages from groups collecting airman outside Brussels reached the *Cantine Suédoise* in a roundabout way. First they were delivered to the house of Elsie's friend, Nelly Deceuninck. Nelly, a girl of eighteen, would take the letters to Elsie at the Maréchals' house in the Avenue Voltaire. They stated laconically that 'parcels' were to be collected at the church. Then Elsie would report to the *Cantine Suédoise* before rushing eagerly to the Square Frère Orban to collect them.

On the morning of 18 November 1942, a sealed green envelope was pushed through the letterbox of the Maréchal home in the Avenue Voltaire in Brussels. Madame Maréchal, who collected it, was mystified, and, thinking it might be intended for Nemo, handed it to her daughter.

'What can it be, Elsie?'

'I expect it is for us to forward on to Paris. We have done this before,' said Elsie.

She put it in her handbag, intending to take it to Nemo at the *Cantine*. Then, curious, she broke the seal and read the tiny slip of paper inside.

'*Deux enfants pour jeudi.*'

Elsie gasped.

'But I don't understand; why has the message come here and not to Nelly?'

Madame Maréchal's brow puckered into a curious frown.

'I must take it to the *Cantine*. The chief will decide what to do.'

Madame Maréchal threw a worried glance at Elsie. She had been under the shadow of the Gestapo from the earliest days, and she and her husband, a civil servant, wished to take no more risks. But they were under the spell of their young daughter's audacious spirit.

On that chill morning an icy wind blew through the Brussels streets in penetrating gusts. The town, in this bleak winter of the war, was shivering and anxious. It required a painful effort to maintain defiance to the enemy, who stamped in field-grey and Luftwaffe blue along the pavements. In the cafés sat Gestapo thugs in civilian clothes, on the watch for the leaders of Comet. Sometimes they would leave hurriedly and follow someone through the crowds.

On 18 November, Albert Mélot was walking quickly to a rendezvous at the Square Frère Orban. Every few paces he looked over his shoulder. Albert was twenty-seven, and for some weeks had been the guide from Namur to Brussels. He had been a scout, and he revelled in the job of guiding airmen.

Behind him walked the two pilots whom he had conducted from Namur. All that Albert knew was that they had been shot down a few days before. Now, dressed as Belgian workers and wearing dark blue berets, they followed the delighted Albert.

As they hurried along the streets, Albert was dimly aware of something wrong. Knowing no English, he could not converse with the men, but their behaviour made him anxious. There was something ominous about the way they moved and spoke.

But it was not far now to the rendezvous at St Joseph's Church, where Elsie Maréchal would question them.

As Albert Mélot reached the church, his suspicions grew. Danger lurked in that windswept square.

The three men stood on the steps of the church for an hour and Elsie did not arrive. Albert listened to the hum of traffic and scanned each figure in the distance. The church clock struck eleven. He watched anxiously for Elsie's schoolgirl figure crossing the square, then waited another half an hour.

His two charges showed impatience as they stamped their feet on the steps of the church. Albert considered whether he should leave them in the church and go in search of Elsie. What had gone wrong?

Perplexed and anxious, he took the two men to the house of Nelly Deceuninck, but Nelly was not at home. Her parents, ignorant of their daughter's underground work, stood bewildered at the door. They gave him the address of the Maréchal family in the Avenue Voltaire.

He rang the bell and, peeping through the curtains, Madame Maréchal and her daughter saw him with his two companions standing outside.

'They are here already. However did they get here?' cried Elsie.

And Albert, still bewildered, explained rapidly in front of the house, as he was in a hurry:

'I did not find anyone at the rendezvous, so I took them to Nelly's house. They gave me your address, and I came here.'

In their front room, Elsie and her mother examined the two young men left by Albert. They were dressed in suits such as ordinary Belgians wore. One, who spoke English with an American accent, was short and dapper. The other was tall, with a long, pale face. Madame Maréchal, proud of her English birth, was delighted to speak to her visitors in their own language. She was doubly pleased to hear that she was the first Belgian to house two American pilots.

'We are Americans serving in the RAF,' they explained.

Excitedly, she went to her kitchen to prepare a meal. But Elsie was uneasy. The men said little. They seemed ill.

'We had a terrible party last night,' said one of them. 'We were drinking whisky.'

Elsie left them to lay the table in the dining room next door. The taller of the men, white in the face, came to the door.

'Can you show me the cabinet?' he said.

Elsie pointed the way to the WC and continued to lay the table. The cabinet! That was a strange word for an American to use. Perhaps, she thought, he is showing off the only word of French he knows!

Bobby, her brother, aged fifteen, came in from school.

Then all five of them – Madame Maréchal, Elsie, Bobby and the Americans – sat down to eat. The visitors looked sick. They had no appetite. Elsie was puzzled.

'You don't look like Americans,' she said suddenly. Everyone was silent. The smaller man looked hard at them. He said abruptly:

'Well, what do we look like?'

'Oh, just like ordinary Belgians.'

When the meal was over, Elsie took them to the front room and set pieces of paper before them.

'Please write your name and numbers – also where you were shot down and in what aircraft.'

They wrote slowly under her gaze. They were nervous and irritable. Elsie took the two pieces of paper and read them. Nemo had impressed on her the need for checking each man carefully. She read, then folded the papers and put them in her handbag. It was time to go to the *Cantine* and report to Nemo.

'Will you give me your English money? It is dangerous to have it on you.'

With an ill grace, they handed over a few shillings.

The taller man rose unsteadily.

'Can we have some fresh air?'

Madame Maréchal replied:

'Yes; why not go in the garden for a minute?'

The men hesitated. The expression on their faces seemed unfriendly.

'No, we would much rather have a good walk.'

'Supposing you cannot find your way back to this house?'

The men's laughter was harsh and unnatural. They could not be persuaded to walk in the tiny back garden.

'Have you ever heard of an American who could not find his way back?' said one of them.

When they had left the house, Elsie remarked to Madame Maréchal that these men were unlike any of the boys of the Royal Air Force they had hidden in the past. Madame Maréchal said reassuringly:

'After all, Elsie, they have come by a regular route. They were brought here by Albert. Americans often look Continental.'

Elsie left the Avenue Voltaire for the *Cantine*. She turned instinctively to see if she was followed, then fell to wondering about the two strange men. They wore khaki shirts, while those of most British airmen were RAF blue. They had written the name of their aircraft as 'Halifax'. She had asked them:

'How many were there in your crew?'

'Four.'

Surely there were more than four men in a Halifax, thought Elsie. But she was too excited to allow her suspicions any rein. She reached the *Cantine Suédoise* at three o'clock in the afternoon and found Nemo with Commandant Bidoul, solemn and anxious. There was bad news from Liège, where many arrests had been made.

Elsie was breathless, her cheeks glowing.

'Splendid news. *Deux enfants!*'

Nemo smiled at her warmly. He had grown thinner these days. He tried to share in her delight.

'Here is the note which we received by the ten o'clock post. It seems that it was delayed. Albert did not find me at the rendezvous, so he took the men straight to Maman, when he found that Nelly was not at home.'

'*Mon Dieu!* How terribly dangerous! Let me look at the note.'

It was written in pencil.

'*Deux enfants pour jeudi.*'

Nemo frowned. The names and the 'd' of the *deux* had more than a suggestion of German script. His suspicions grew and then slowly receded as he listened to Elsie.

He showed the note to Peggy and Commandant Bidoul, who looked serious.

'I don't like this, Elsie. Have you questioned them yet?'

'Only a little. There has not been time. I thought it best to bring the note to you.' Elsie was still far from the black suspicion which lurked in Nemo's thoughts.

He rose and grimly paced the room, and as he did so Elsie felt suddenly cold and afraid.

'Elsie, you must go back immediately,' he said quietly. 'Stop these men from leaving again at all costs. Interrogate them carefully. Then come back. If you suspect them, your mother and you must leave the house immediately.'

They faced each other, the schoolgirl and the Baron. A hundred speculations roamed in Nemo's mind. Had it come at last? But why this occasion more than another?

Elsie ran from the office and down the Rue Ducale to take the tram.

The two men brought by Albert Mélot kept their word, and within an hour returned to the house in the Avenue Voltaire. Madame Maréchal had finished washing up and went to talk to them in the front room.

'What part of America do you come from?'

The tall, pale man answered:

'New Jersey.'

There was a strange inflection in his speech, and Madame Maréchal resolved that as soon as Elsie returned she would send her back to warn the chief.

The men had grown silent. Madame Maréchal wondered what to say. She was surprised that Americans should talk so little.

The bell rang and she rose to open the front door. In the passage the tall man pushed past her and dashed towards it. Madame Maréchal felt her arm seized from behind. She was swung round. The other man held a revolver.

He spoke to her with his twisted smile:

'Madame, the game is up!'

Poor Madame Maréchal raised her arms. The open front door revealed a man in a raincoat, wearing glasses. She found herself sitting once more in one of her armchairs, with a macabre group round her. The three of them questioned her.

'Where has your daughter gone?'

'Who is your chief?'

'Where is his headquarters?'

Madame Maréchal fought desperately for time. She thought of her husband, and Elsie and young Bobby. Was there any means of warning them? The three men watched her every movement. They searched her. Then the newcomer in the rain-coat said sharply:

'Get your hat and coat.'

He followed her to her bedroom with a drawn revolver, then pushed her roughly along the passage to the front door. A car waited outside.

Nemo had given Elsie his own suitcase and filled it with food from the store of the *Cantine Suédoise* to feed the supposed Americans. He implored her to be careful of it.

'*J'y tiens comme à la prunelle de mes yeux,*' he said.

Elsie sat in the tram with the suitcase. The thrill of adventure, of helping 'Americans', had overcome her fears. She thought that their strange behaviour could be explained by the whisky they had drunk.

She reached the house in the Avenue Voltaire and rang the bell.

The door seemed to open of its own accord, very slowly.

Could it be a joke? Elsie jumped into the passage. A revolver was pointed at her stomach. The smaller of the two 'Americans' laughed venomously.

'Well, Elsie! The game is up. Please keep quiet.'

He pushed open the door of the dining room. There, eight men sat drinking tea. The air was heavy with cigar smoke. They ordered her to sit in the midst of a circle of cruel faces.

'You'd better talk, Elsie. Your mother didn't want to, and something happened to her in the kitchen.'

One of them searched her handbag. He took out a piece of paper, and Elsie clutched at her throat. It was a certificate signed by Nemo to say that she was working at the *Cantine Suédoise*. He had given it to her to help avoid deportation to Germany, with which all young Belgians of eighteen and over were threatened.

The German did not seem interested. He put the paper back in her bag.

They took Elsie to an office in the Rue de la Traversière and questioned her till ten o'clock that night, when her father and Bobby were brought in. Poor Monsieur Maréchal, after a long day in Flanders, had returned, tired out, to the Avenue Voltaire, and there met the same fate as all his family.

Nemo, waiting at the *Cantine Suédoise* for Elsie's return, nervously drummed his fingers on his desk. From the corridors of the *Cantine* came the happy laughter of children and the patter of their feet on the steps as they scampered into the street. The shadows lengthened on the grass among the trees of the Rue Ducale. It was growing dark, and Elsie had not returned.

The silence was terrible. It was as if the heart of Nemo's little organisation had nearly stopped beating. The clock ticked impersonally as Commandant Bidoul started to gather up his papers for the night. Peggy sat as usual on the arm of a chair. As she turned her head and listened for the sound of footsteps, the sunset caught her red hair. She walked to the window and stared out.

Only young Victor Michiels, alias Louis, a new recruit to the *Cantine*, still kept up a cheerful conversation. He was twenty-five and athletic. Generous and intelligent, he implored Nemo to let him go and investigate.

It was now dark outside, and only the passing light of a torch showed in the blackout of the street.

'Yes, go and spy out the land,' said Nemo. 'See if you notice anything suspicious about the house. For God's sake don't get too close.'

Nemo, looking at him, wondered if he had warned him

sufficiently of what might be lying in wait at the house in the Avenue Voltaire.

'On no account try to go into the house, Louis, unless you are absolutely certain that there is no danger.'

'I won't. I'll be very careful.'

He shook hands and, still smiling, left the room. Peggy and Nemo heard the door bang and his footsteps faded into the distance.

Victor, with an agreeable sensation of adventure, took the same route that Elsie had followed that fatal afternoon. He could see little in the dim blue light of the tram, until it clanged to a halt near the Avenue Voltaire. Brown leaves rustled. It was a cold, still evening. The houses stood faintly outlined in the darkness. Victor turned up the collar of his overcoat and waited under a tree.

Half an hour passed. Outside the house of the Maréchal family nothing was to be seen or heard save occasional footsteps in the Avenue. Straining his ears, Victor could hear no voices, no click of a gate latch.

Victor struggled with his fears and his impatience. The wind had risen again, so that he could no longer hear anything distinctly. He walked slowly to the house and stood listening.

There was no movement or noise. Only the windows seemed to look blindly down at him.

Footsteps were coming towards him, and he began to walk calmly in their direction. An officer and a girl walked past him, talking in German. They did not seem to notice him.

Victor, relieved, returned calmly to the door and rang the bell.

There was a click. Then a movement around him as if he had disturbed some fearful animal in the darkness. A torch flashed.

'Halt!'

Three German Field policemen stood there. Each had a revolver. Victor saw a face beneath a helmet. He backed a few paces, holding his hands above his head.

Again came a cry of 'Halt!'

Victor decided. He had a quick vision of the roadway he had seen at dusk with a turning from the Avenue Voltaire quite close. It was very dark. It was worth trying.

He turned and bounded towards the turning. He must have covered several yards before he heard the first shot, and in the same moment felt the shock of the bullet. He heard the second shot as he still ran. A tremendous force seemed to block his path and draw him down amid red, searing flames. Then the third bullet shook his body and night folded him to her soft wings.

A dog barked. The leaves rustled in the gutter. There was the clamour of German voices. In the beam of the torch, three steel-helmeted figures stood over the sprawling body. The light shone in the slow river of blood. And Nemo, looking anxiously at his watch in his silent office at the *Cantine Suédoise*, heard the mourning of the wind. He shrugged his shoulders, picked up his Eden hat, and hurried home to Zellick.

## Chapter Nine

# Peggy

When dawn broke on the morning of 19 November, mist hung over bare trees in the parks of Brussels. A red sun rose above the city, and frost lined the windows of the houses in the Avenue Voltaire. A few paces from the front door of the Maréchals' house, there was still blood on the pavement.

An old man, walking slowly with his dog, looked at the evidence of the previous night and sighed. He had heard the three staccato shots and the shouts of the Germans. At least, he thought, death must have come swiftly.

Peggy, who had left the *Cantine Suédoise* with Nemo to return to Hal, had hardly slept. She had been expecting Victor to telephone. As she lay awake, waiting, and there was no call from him, she began to fear the worst. She dared not telephone his home. She knew, too, that Elvire Morelle would arrive from Paris at five o'clock in the morning and would go straight to the Maréchals.

Peggy thought of this with horror. There was nothing she could do to warn Elvire. At that hour there were no trams, and the curfew imposed by the Germans lasted till seven in the morning.

At nine o'clock she left her home. Her sense of approaching tragedy grew to a definite fear. Something would happen that same day. She packed her largest handbag, a toothbrush, a change of linen, some sugar and money.

When she arrived at the *Cantine Suédoise*, Nemo and Georges d'Oultremont anxiously paced the floor of the office. There was no news. Elsie and Victor had disappeared completely. No one would risk a telephone call to Victor's family, in case the wires were tapped. Yet his home was only three doors away from the *Cantine* in the Rue Ducale.

Peggy was eager to act.

'Nemo,' she said, 'I will go and see what has happened. I know Victor's sister. She is studying at Louvain University. If there is anyone there, I shall say I have come to discuss details of her course in philosophy, for I intend to go to that University myself.'

Nemo's face wore an anxious frown. He was pale and worried.

'I do not like this, Peggy. Victor would surely have got in touch with us if he was at liberty. You will run into a trap.'

Peggy laughed and tossed her red head.

'I shall be all right. I have an alibi. I will be back soon.'

She left the *Cantine* through the shabby garden at the back, opening a gate in the wall with an enormous key. She found herself in a street which ran parallel with the Rue Ducale and walked to its end, changing her direction until she came to a large white house, the home of the Michiels. She walked boldly up to the white porch and rang the bell. At the moment she did so, she suspected she was trapped. The door opened immediately. The familiar trim parlour maid was not there, as usual, to welcome her. A tall, cadaverous man, with deep-set eyes of the darkest blue, stood before her.

'Come in, *Mademoiselle*,' he said in a sepulchral voice.

When she had entered, he turned suddenly to Peggy:

'What do you want?'

Peggy nerved herself to give the answer she had prepared.

'I have come to see Josée Michiels.'

The lean man seized her arm and, throwing open the door of the drawing room, pushed her in. She found herself in a silent circle of people. Slowly she recognised familiar faces. There were Victor's parents and his sister, Josée. The circle was completed by two Germans. Then she realised her folly. She thought of Nemo and the anxiety that her disappearance would cause him after the crisis of the last twenty-four hours. She must bluff her way out at all costs.

The Germans questioned her. One of them snatched her handbag and extracted several photographs.

'What are these?'

'All those are photographs of a German family I knew before the war.'

The Germans looked baffled. Peggy, by some sixth sense, had taken the precaution of putting these photographs in her bag before leaving home. She assumed an air of innocence, and spoke in excellent German of her holidays in Germany.

They were nonplussed. They turned the conversation to the Michiels family. How did she know them?

'I only know Josée.'

'But you know Victor Michiels, don't you?'

'No,' said Peggy firmly. 'I know neither of her brothers.'

'We do not believe you, *Mademoiselle*. We must take you to our office for interrogation.'

Time passed slowly in the pleasant drawing room. The spirits of the prisoners slowly revived, and they started a game of bridge.

Peggy, putting her hand in the pocket of her dress, felt the key of the garden gate of the *Cantine*, and slipped it beneath the cushion of her chair. They lunched in the drawing room, everyone trying to be cheerful and normal. Only Monsieur Michiels, the father of Victor, was sad and silent. Sometimes his voice would falter. He alone knew that his son was dead.

In the afternoon, Peggy was taken in a German car to be interrogated at a house near the Parc du Cinquantaire. Beside her sat a close-cropped German, his dark felt hat low over his forehead. He said:

'You may as well know we had to shoot young Michiels last night.'

'Oh, it is not possible!' cried Peggy.

She realised immediately her mistake. She had claimed not to have known him. But the German, who seemed unaccountably disturbed by the young man's death, did not appear to have noticed. He turned to her:

'If you dare say anything about this, things will go badly for you.'

At length Peggy found herself in a grim waiting room among other prisoners. None of them was a member of the Comet Line. She braced herself for the meeting with Elsie. She expected to see her small, dark figure enter at any moment. For she was certain that Elsie had been arrested.

Peggy waited for more than an hour, and then came a summons to the next room. She passed a tall, fair woman in the doorway. Neither of them made any sign of recognition. At first, Peggy did not clearly understand who it was. Then she felt a sudden pang of horror. Of course, it was Elvire Morelle!

A few hours earlier, Elvire had arrived from Paris. Her mission was to search for airmen. She carried with her a small suitcase, a parcel and a handbag. She was hatless, with her hair untidy. Her parcel contained food for her brother, Charlie, still in the prison of St Gilles.

She paused as she approached the fatal house in the Avenue Voltaire. A Belgian *garde civile* was pacing the roadway. Was there something wrong? The *garde* stopped and stood motionless. She reached the gate. She had not seen the blood on the pavement. She rang the bell.

The door opened and a huge German stood in the hall. At his belt was a black revolver holster, unbuttoned. He drew the revolver and pointed it at her.

'Secret Police of the Luftwaffe,' he said in guttural French. 'So we have yet another visitor?'

Elvire fought for time.

'Pardon, *Monsieur*, I do not understand you.'

'Do not move!'

Two more Germans appeared. The man with the revolver motioned her into the front room. The others seized the suitcase, the parcel and her handbag. The objects were thrown roughly on a table. Elvire felt suddenly faint and then recovered herself quickly. How idiotic to have been caught in this way! What madness to have approached the house after she had seen the *garde civile* outside!

In the front room, full of stale cigar smoke, the Germans began their interrogation. Glasses and bottles stood untidily among the treasures of poor Madame Maréchal. In the kitchen, where less than twenty-four hours earlier she had happily prepared to entertain the 'Americans', a German was making coffee.

After a short questioning, Elvire was handcuffed and led to a waiting lorry, where she sat between two Germans. The parcel which she had brought for her brother was flung in after her. Elvire determined at all costs to stand firm.

The lorry jolted and swayed over the tramlines, and she thought with deep anxiety of Elsie and her family. Had Nemo been arrested? It was a heart-rending moment. At all costs Dédée and Paul must be warned. The Line must continue.

Elvire prayed for strength to face this dreaded hour. The Germans, sitting beside her, had expressionless faces. They would never understand her infinite patience. Like Little Cyclone, she had a passionate, maternal devotion to the work of the Comet Line. She believed with all her heart that the rescue of Allied airmen from the Germans was an act of Christian duty. It was a cause beside which the fear of death had lost its meaning. Within her was a sacrificial courage. Her only fears were for her friends who were in danger. She had none for herself.

The lorry stopped and Elvire, handcuffed, was assisted to the pavement. She looked at the sun, now risen above the mist, and wondered when she would see it again as a free woman. She was hungry and tired, but unafraid.

A German grasped her elbow and pushed her roughly up the steps of a block of offices, with the notice 'Secret Police of the Luftwaffe'. She was led, like a naughty child, into a big room where an officer in Luftwaffe uniform sat at a table. There were files spread out before him and the familiar scent of stale cigar smoke.

'Sit down.'

The room had a Prussian neatness – maps, filing cabinets, trestle tables. Above the desk hung a large, scowling photograph of the Führer and, to one side, a portrait of Göring, in a white uniform, holding the jewelled baton of *Reichmarschall.*

Why had she been brought to the headquarters of the Luftwaffe? Elvire was soon to realize that the Luftwaffe regarded escape organisations as their special province. They knew better than anyone the value of a rescued airman.

Elvire's suitcase was lifted on to the table with Charlie's parcel and her handbag. The German methodically searched among her few clothes, opened the parcel without apparent interest, then turned his attention to the handbag. He opened it, took out a comb, a mirror and a prayerbook. A folded piece of flimsy paper fell from his hand.

For the first time that morning fear came to Elvire. She clasped her hands, no longer manacled, in silent prayer. A terrible thought passed through her mind. She saw the Rue Oudinot at evening with a German car drawn up beside the doorway of Paul's *appartement*. The Gestapo were climbing the stairs to the third floor and hammering on the door. She saw Paul and Dédée led, like herself, to a waiting car... Then Aimable, then Robert and Germaine... The Line would be lost, the sacrifices would have been in vain.

She passed her hand across her forehead, trying desperately not to appear interested in the folded paper, for it was a copy of the lease in her name of the *appartement* in the Rue Oudinot.

The German officer seemed uninterested in the paper. He turned to a filing cabinet, thus standing with his back to Elvire. She did not hesitate. With lightning speed, she seized the paper, screwed it into a ball and quickly swallowed it. The German officer saw nothing. He did not notice the passing of that valuable document.

In this same room only a few hours before, the Germans had begun their interrogation of the Maréchals. For the rest of that terrible November, and for weeks afterwards, they brought Elsie and her parents before them. They beat and cajoled them, but always the family refused to reveal a single detail. Yet slowly Elsie realised that the secret of the *Cantine Suédoise* was known. She was called one day to a plain, enormous room. A short, pale German sat studying her with narrowed eyes. He seemed to Elsie like a large rat. He spoke in a thin, unpleasant voice:

'Who is this Nemo? Is he the director of the *Cantine Suédoise*?'

'I do not know.'

'But you admit you worked there?'

And so the interminable interrogation went on. Sometimes it lasted a day and into the night. At intervals, the Luftwaffe Police, reinforced by the Gestapo, beat this eighteen-year-old girl until she was covered with bruises and unable to lie on her back for weeks. The proud Luftwaffe had sunk far in shame. Sometimes she was led half-fainting to her cell in the prison of St Gilles. All night long the prisoners could hear her heartbreaking sobs. Yet her bitter tears were not for the weals and bruises on her own young body. They were for Nemo and his friends, whom she was powerless to warn.

On the evening of 19 November, Peggy was taken to a house opposite that where she had met Elvire. She was questioned by the same fat German who had interrogated Elsie. His eyes narrowed as he watched her.

Peggy was determined to talk her way out. She spoke in German, which impressed him.

But the questions continued. Did she know Victor Michiels? How did she know his sister? Why did she want to see her? Where did she learn German?

Late that evening she won over the small fat man and the German who had accompanied her in the car. The *Cantine* was not mentioned, nor was Elsie or the false Americans. When it was past eight o'clock, she was taken across the road to the other house and there released.

'I can go, can I?' she exclaimed. She nearly gave herself away in her excitement.

'*Ach, naturlich!*'

Peggy, still surprised, shook the Gestapo officer by the hand and left the house alone. When she had gone 100 yards she burst into tears. Then she began to walk, filled with a wonderful sense of freedom. Sometimes she looked over her shoulder to see if she was being followed. Then, coming to a church, she went inside and prayed.

From the church she went to a friend's house and telephoned to Nemo. To the anxious Nemo her voice sounded as if she were a ghost. In a guarded way he told her of the savage work of the false Americans. For these two dangerous agents of the enemy had penetrated the whole Line from the Ardennes and Namur to the very centre of his organisation in Brussels. In two days, nearly 100 people, all helpers of the Line, were arrested. Some were guides, some shelterers, some innocent relatives thrown into prison as hostages. Of these, many would never see their homes again. Such was the price paid by the Comet Line for the return of sixty airmen in the past six months.

Peggy arrived late at her home at Hal on the outskirts of Brussels. Her brother was astonished to see her drink three glasses of wine.

'What has happened to you today?' he asked.

'Oh, nothing,' said Peggy. 'I have been rather busy.'

## Chapter Ten

# Urrugne

At the Rue Vaneau in Paris, Paul smoothed his hair, now almost white, and went on stamping forged identity cards. He felt suddenly old and unable to keep pace with the exuberance of the young. For them terror had not the same meaning. In their active lives they had no time for the morbid thoughts which tormented him. Perhaps the old could become a danger to the young by planting in their minds the seed of fear?

All his free moments were given up to thoughts of Dédée. She had always been a little cyclone. He recalled the child, bright-eyed and laughing, a determined character. She had wished to be a boy. To her, he had never been able to refuse anything.

'There is one agony', he thought as he sat alone at the Rue Vaneau, 'which is worse than death at the hands of the Gestapo. It is my fear for Dédée. Will she return from Spain?'

His instinct told him that he was becoming a danger to her. He knew that she was the motive force that had given him, the quiet schoolmaster of nearly sixty, a love of adventure. He ran the risks cheerfully, believing firmly in Dédée's cause and its ultimate success. It was to rid his country and France, to whom he had become deeply attached, of the tyranny of Hitler.

Dédée and her father were united in a passion for justice. The Comet Line was built on equality, though many of their

comrades came from aristocratic Belgian families. Such were
Nemo, and the d'Oultremonts and Franco. No one served the
cause with any thought of rank. There was a camaraderie, a
loyalty unto death. In the four years of the Line, there were
thousands, many poor and humble in back streets and little
farms, who risked their lives to hide the airmen. To Dédée and
Paul, their organisation was the realisation of a dream in which
all worked without favour or thought of the future. For those
who were to face the levelled rifles of the SS, this faith lasted to
the end.

The news of the calamity at Brussels had reached Paul at
the Rue Vaneau in Paris. The enemy was on every side of him.
He was the person for whom the Gestapo was searching. He
was Enemy Number One. Since those fatal days when the
bogus Americans had wrought such damage, the price upon his
head had been doubled. The Gestapo and the Luftwaffe Secret
Police had long convinced themselves that he and he alone was
the chief of the Comet Line.

At the end of December, he witnessed the departure for
England of Peggy and Georges and Edouard d'Oultremont.
Peggy had seen crowded hours in the service of Nemo, but it
was time for her to flee. As she travelled to the frontier, her
thoughts were only of Nemo and the black perils that gathered
round him.

In England, she stepped from the aircraft which brought
her from Gibraltar and confronted the man whom she was later
to marry.

Beside the aircraft from which she alighted stood a
Coldstream Guards' officer with an empty sleeve. He was
Jimmy Langley MBE, MC, who was wounded and captured in

France in 1940 and escaped a year later, after his arm had been amputated.

Peggy, one of the luckiest survivors of the Line, lives today with her four children in an old house in peaceful Suffolk.[†]

The doorbell rang twice, and Paul, concealing his identity cards and stamps, hurried to open it. Dédée was there, smiling, in his arms. Her twenty-fourth journey from Paris to Bilbao was safely over. She had now led 118 men over the Pyrenees. In all, thirty-three crossings had been made, seven by 'B' Johnson.

She flung her satchel on a chair. It was a cold, rainy night, and her hair and clothes were wet. She drank a glass of wine. She sat there, dainty and alert in spite of her weariness.

'What has happened, Father?'

'No more news from Brussels; but all is quiet here.'

'Robert seems to be managing well. The Paris Line seems assured for the moment.'

'Yes.' There was silence. Paul knew she was going to say something important.

'You mean that I must leave?'

'Yes, Father, you are bound to be caught in time.'

'I hate the idea of leaving you.'

But on the morrow he decided to go with the next party. Perhaps it was the counsel of his friend, Robert Aylé. Perhaps he knew that for Dédée his presence beside her was an embarrassment. Intrepid, masterful, as she was, still she was afraid for him. If he was safe, she could the better face the dangers of her task.

They left Paris on the evening of 13 January 1943: Paul,

---

[†]    Peggy Langley died on 20 July 2000.

Dédée, Franco and three pilots. All three were airman from the Royal Air Force; one was American, two were British. Paul had left the flat in the Rue Vaneau with a heavy heart. He looked round the cheerless rooms for the last time.

The crowded train sped on through the bleak January night. Paul sat in his corner, unable to sleep.

A heavy rainstorm swept Bayonne as they arrived. The passengers made their way to their rendezvous with Tante Go. They followed her to a café and there sat grimly listening to her news.

Tante Go was serious. The plan to take Paul over to Spain was impossible. The rain for days past had been tropical. From Florentino she had heard that the Bidassoa would be quite impassable for a week.

'*Monsieur le professeur,*' she said to Paul, 'at your age it cannot be done. You cannot do the extra five hours' march and cross the bridge. In the mountains the rain and the wind will be terrible. You will not survive.'

La Tante was commanding.

'Dédée must take the men over alone, and her father must wait here until the rains have subsided. Then he can cross the river.'

It was agreed that Franco, no longer needed on this journey, should return to Paris to prepare another party for escape to Spain.

Paul surrendered. He was bitterly disappointed. He had longed to cross the mountains once with Dédée, to say goodbye to her in the safety of a neutral country.

Outside the station, he embraced his daughter. The rain had soaked his beret and ran down his cheeks.

'Goodbye, my darling. I shall come with you next time.'

He had a blurred vision of her leaving, as, led by Tante Go, the party set off on bicycles through the pelting rain for St Jean de Luz.

The road from St Jean de Luz to Francia's farm at Urrugne had become a river of mud. The torrential rain blinded the party as they climbed the steep slopes above the bay. It was impossible to hear anything above the roar of the storm. All were wet to the skin. Their boots sank into the slush of cart-tracks or slipped on the moss-covered stones.

Dédée sensed, though she could neither see nor hear in that raging downpour, that Florentino was anxious. She was familiar with the road, but never in her experience had a storm of such violence broken over the mountain.

At last they came to Francia's farmhouse and stepped into the orange light of the kitchen. They could hear the rain beating savagely against the windowpanes. Inside all was warm and inviting. Glasses of hot milk and soup were set before them. The airmen looked around and saw the neat, white room, the polished brass. Soon they were playing with Francia's three dark-eyed children, content and disdainful of the tempest outside.

Florentino sat, with his beret perched on his head, talking in his own Basque language to Francia. The lamplight glowed on the figures at the table. The airmen, drinking wine, were lost in happy laughter with the children. Above them in the shadows hung a plaster crucifix.

Dédée and Florentino were grave. It was impossible to pass over the frontier in that thick, black, tempestuous night. Not even the most experienced guide – and no one knew the way like Florentino – could attempt the crossing without courting disaster.

Dédée must accept Florentine's decision and wait with the

men until the following evening. The door was blown open by the force of the wind, and the occupants of the kitchen could hear its roar as it flung the rain in. Then Florentino, who decided to return to his home at Ciboure, waved his hand and disappeared into the howling night.

The travellers were tired, and, as a pleasant drowsiness overtook them, they climbed steep wooden stairs to the trim bedrooms above. When morning broke, the storm had subsided, though a forbidding grey mist covered the mountaintops and a drizzle fell over the fields. Small torrents rushed from the hills.

Dédée and the men fit and able to march the extra five hours would make the journey that evening by crossing the suspension bridge at Puigcerdá. All morning, the Americans and the two British airmen joked together and drank coffee made by the good Francia. A savoury smell of soup pervaded the farmhouse, and soon they were drinking and eating in the mood of gay expectancy which often overtakes men about to set out on an adventure into the unknown. For them it was the last lap. They were confident of freedom.

Dédée herself, though annoyed by the delay, felt relieved and free from the doubts and fears of past months. Paul would soon be able to cross. He would be safe in Britain, and the worry about him would be over. It was not that she felt that he was too old to work in the Line. His kindly guidance had often saved her and her young friends from disaster. It was just that she could not bear to think of him defenceless against the cunning enemy. She knew that but for his devotion to her and her cause he would never have involved himself in such dangerous work.

In the distance was a faint whirr of an engine. As the sound drew closer to the farmhouse, the merriment suddenly stopped.

No one expressed alarm. Even in that remote place, cars would pass occasionally. The sound of the engine ceased.

'The Gestapo!' said the Americans, taking out a sheath knife and pointing it in schoolboy fashion towards the door. There was general laughter. No one showed fear.

A dark shadow moved across the window of the farmhouse.

Dédée rose. She had seen the dark blue *képi* of a *gendarme*. Quickly she motioned the men upstairs. She was too late. The door burst open, and in the pale grey light were the figures of two *gendarmes*. Their *mitraillettes* covered the group at the table.

All were now standing, pale and silent. The steam still rose from the soup bowls. The children gathered round their mother. A dog barked outside.

'Keep your hands above your heads!'

'Turn to the wall.'

Ten *gendarmes* invaded the kitchen. They were big, burly men. Most carried rifles. Dédée, Francia and the pilots were led into the farmyard, while the house was searched from the cellar to the lofts. Every piece of furniture, every picture was thrown aside. The floorboards were lifted, even the hay was combed.

'Where is Florentino? Is he hiding here?'

None of the captives, standing in the farmyard mud, would answer.

'You will talk, my friends. You will talk.'

They were a wretched group, their gaiety and high spirits suddenly gone. The children began to cry.

After the first shock had left her, Dédée began to think quickly. How had the *gendarmes* found the farmhouse of Francia? Had there been treachery?

Even to this day there are no certain details of this betrayal, for betrayal it was. In St Jean de Luz and Ciboure one hears tales. Some say there was time to warn the party in the farm-house, for the *gendarmes* had been seen preparing for their coup earlier in the day. Whoever was the traitor, this denunciation left three small children motherless, for Francia Usandizanga was to die in the stinking corruption of Ravensbrück on 12 April 1945.

The rain began to fall once more on this fatal 15 January. Dédée and her companions shivered under the guard of two *gendarmes*. An hour passed. Then sharp orders were given and a strange procession began to descend the winding road to St Jean de Luz. It was the road which Dédée and her parties of escapers had used so often to reach Urrugne.

The men were marched in single file, their hands clasped at the backs of their heads. Behind came Dédée, still dressed in her blue trousers and *espadrilles*, her hair wet with rain, and poor Francia of Urrugne, pale and horror-struck. On each side marched a line of five *gendarmes*, their rifles *à l'épaule*. Their heavy boots rang on the road.

The procession continued over the bridge which divides Ciboure from St Jean de Luz and came to a halt at the *bureau de police*. There was a rapid interrogation, and before it was dusk the women and the three pilots were locked in the cells of the town prison.

The news came to Anglet that evening. Already Florentino had started over the mountains to warn the British in Bilbao that Dédée had been caught. In St Jean de Luz, many a heart went cold at the thought of the young girl fallen into the hands of the enemy. On that night it seemed that the powers of darkness had won a victory and that the guiding spirit of the Line had been snatched away.

Tante Go's first action was to try to comfort Paul, who was prostrate with grief and remorse. He ran his hands through his white hair in his anguish as he sat at a table in her villa at Anglet.

The apparently endless storm buffeted the windows. Paul's eyes, filled with tears, seemed not to see, not to hear the restrained condolences of Tante Go, 'B' and Janine.

All that long night he dreamed of her in the prison of St Jean de Luz. His tortured imagination saw her lying in her cell. It was hard to believe that one so young and shining, so courageous, should have been taken. The moment he had dreaded for so long had come.

## Chapter Eleven

# Villa Chagrin

In this bitter disaster, Tante Go showed the finest qualities. Her fierce green eyes flashing, she rounded on the faint hearts:

'All is not lost. We can still rescue her before the Boches find out her real identity.'

On the evening of 16 January 1943, Dédée was transferred from St Jean de Luz to the Villa Chagrin at Bayonne. Villa Chagrin! An apt name for this gloomy prison! It lies beneath a railway embankment, and its yellow, squat buildings can be seen from the Paris train. Around it is a high wall. Trees shelter this lonely, sinister place. Even its southern colours, its red roofs and green shutters, fail to soften its grim face.

While Dédée lay in her cell, the active brain of Tante Go conjured plans for her escape. The days passed in anxious discussion at the villa at Anglet. Paul, for his own safety, was sent into hiding at the house of her loyal friend, Jean Dassié. Tante Go decided this was imperative, for he had made a bold but senseless visit to the prison. For forty-eight hours there had been no certain news of the identity of the young girl arrested in the mountains. That it was Dédée was discovered by the stalwart Jean Dassié, who was chief telephone operator at the Bayonne Exchange. He had overheard the details of the disaster at Urrugne, and hurried to tell Tante Go.

On the 14th, 'B' Johnson had gone to Francia's farm to

collect the identity cards of the escaping airmen. This duty he performed so that the false names could be used once more with different photographs. When he reached the farm all was silent. The wind whistled mournfully about the stone walls and the seagulls cried above the fields. The house was locked and empty. Only a bewildered woman from a neighbouring farm could he find. She was too stupefied to explain to him what had happened. This news and Jean Dassié's report of his overheard telephone conversation confirmed the news.

When the first shock was over, Paul, too, showed wonderful courage. While he remained in hiding at Jean Dassié's house, he could not bear to think of his daughter's plight. Each day he would insist that some dramatic rescue attempt be made. He did not have long to wait.

For Tante Go was in her element. At no time did she lose her head. She chose for her headquarters the Bar Gachy, a *bistro* opposite the gloomy walls of Villa Chagrin. It was here that only a few days before Dédée and the airmen had laughed happily as they drank a cup of coffee on the way from Paris to Urrugne. The *patron* of this humble place was a staunch supporter of the Line. In his back room Tante Go laid her plans.

'Do you know any of the French *gardiens, Monsieur le patron*?'

'Yes. Several come here in the evenings.'

'Do you know one you can trust to help us in something really dangerous?'

The *patron* sipped his coffee and looked hard at Tante Go.

'Yes, I believe I do. He will come here tomorrow. If you are here then, perhaps we may talk.'

Tante Go was gone like a whirlwind, rallying her supporters as she hurried from house to house in Bayonne, Anglet and St

Jean de Luz. Next day she returned on her bicycle to the Bar Gachy, with 'B' Johnson. A *gardien* of the prison was sitting there, a large, rubicund Frenchman.

'Madame, we have an idea,' said the *patron*.

'Go on,' said Tante Go.

The *patron* pointed to a row of vast soup containers standing against the wall of the kitchen.

'We cook the soup for the prisoners here and it is carried across to the Villa. Do you think that the young lady could hide in one of these?'

'I should think so,' said Tante Go. 'She is not very big.'

The genial warder hesitated.

'This will not be easy. We shall need more than one person inside the prison to help us. Though nearly all the staff are French, I cannot trust them.'

Tante Go listened with rapt attention. She realised from his talk that Dédée had not yet fallen into the hands of the Gestapo. She must act quickly.

The warder spoke again.

'It is urgent, Madame, that something should be done before the Boches begin to take too much interest.'

Tante Go understood.

'It would take some time and preparation to get her into one of the empty containers?'

'Yes, I am afraid so.'

'Then we must think of something else. Could you leave a door open?'

'Yes, I will try that. Be here at three o'clock tomorrow. If I can get her out before the Germans come, you must take her away from this district immediately.'

On the following afternoon, Tante Go, 'B' Johnson and Jean Dassié sat in the little café furtively watching the prison gates across the roadway. Half an hour passed and no one came. Suddenly there was the screech of brakes, and a German car pulled up before the prison.

'We are too late,' murmured Tante Go sadly. 'They are taking her away.'

They waited, trying to avoid the suspicious glances of a young SS driver who strutted before the window in his long field-grey overcoat, fingering the black revolver holster at his belt.

Ten minutes passed. The prison gates opened again and two agents of the Gestapo led Dédée out to the waiting car. She was still in trousers and *espadrilles*, her costume for crossing the Pyrenees, which she had been wearing when she was arrested at Urrugne. In the distance she looked pale, but she walked with her head erect and, speaking to neither of her guards, entered the car and was driven away.

It was twenty-four hours before Tante Go and her organisation realised what had happened. The Gestapo had taken her to their local headquarters in Bayonne for interrogation, and returned her to the prison that same evening after dark.

There was still time to act. The greatest danger lay in the behaviour of Paul, who had once more emerged from his hiding place, and clamoured for action. Tante Go spoke to him sharply. She advised him to cross into Spain to discuss the possibility of intervening with the Germans to save his daughter's life.

'But at all costs the Germans must not link Dédée with you. If they do, it will certainly be death for you both.'

Tante Go spoke with such intensity that Paul, despite his grief, was persuaded to return to his hiding place in Jean Dassié's house. He must await a chance to go to Spain.

Tante Go, searching for new helpers, made the acquaintance of a Frenchwoman working for the Red Cross. She was known as Madame 'X'. This good lady paid regular visits to the prisons of the region. She had lost a son fighting the Germans. She was allowed to visit Dédée in her cell, but she was reluctant to take the risk of carrying messages. It was, however, possible for Tante Go to smuggle small pieces of paper in a loaf of bread and a warm, woollen skirt which Madame 'X' carried to Dédée. A file and a hacksaw blade hidden in a cake were intercepted by the prison staff. In the messages which reached her, Dédée learned that her father was in hiding and still safe. This gave her courage to face further interrogation. It was clear to her that the Germans, had, as yet, little information about her.

From harassed Madame 'X', Tante Go learned that Dédée's cell was in a part of the prison close to the outer wall. It might be possible to reach her by climbing this wall. For several days feverish consultations took place. Franco had come from Paris to join the rescue party. Franco with 'B' Johnson and Jean Dassié prepared a contrivance of ropes and grappling hooks to fix to the top of the prison wall. This plan was impracticable, for even if one or more of the rescuers got into the main courtyard, they had no idea how Dédée could be extricated from her cell.

After waiting several nights for a waning moon, Tante Go and the three men carried their contraption in the darkness to the Villa Chagrin. Franco hoisted the grappling hooks into the air at the end of a poke, but it reached only halfway up the wall. There had been a disastrous miscalculation.

A hurried, whispered conference and Jean Dassié disappeared. He returned in half an hour and, to Tante Go's delight, brought with him a long builder's ladder which he had borrowed from a nearby barn. They were luckier with this, because it reached three-quarters of the way up the wall.

Jean Dassié had performed a signal feat in getting the ladder to the prison at all. He had only one arm. He had lost the other in 'Quatorze' (1940). France climbed the ladder first, followed by 'B' Johnson. While Franco, on the top rung of the ladder, was vainly endeavouring to reach the top of the wall with the heavy grappling hooks, there was the familiar sound of jack-boots. A German patrol marched towards them.

Franco, with 'B' Johnson just below him, pressed themselves against the wall to take advantage of the shadows. At the foot of the ladder Jean Dassié flung his voluminous black cloak around Tante Go, thus concealing the foot of the ladder from the Germans who were now passing within a few yards of them. The waning moon had obligingly passed behind a cloud, concealing Franco and 'B' on the ladder, but faintly revealing Jean Dassié and Tante Go locked in an embrace under the protective cloak.

Even the Germans, marching in the crisp night air, could appreciate this nocturnal love scene *à l'éspagnole*, and discreetly turned their heads. They marched stolidly out of sight round the corner of the prison wall. Middle-aged Jean Dassié, who had watched them with apprehension, heaved a sigh of relief as their footsteps died away and released the chuckling Tante Go from his embrace.

To Franco, who had been struggling with the weight of the grappling hooks, the incident was interminable, and to 'B' Johnson, who had been struggling to hold Franco in position.

The only concrete result of this bold but unsuccessful attempt was that Franco from the top of the ladder had discovered a second wall twelve feet high which would have to be climbed.

Disconsolately, the Tante and her party trooped back with their ropes, grappling hooks and builder's ladder to Jean Dassié's house. They passed the spot on the banks of the River Adour, where a boat was to have ferried the rescued Dédée across to a waiting motor car.

Undaunted, Tante Go called a council of war early next morning. She realised that before any further attempts were made to rescue Dédée, they required more information about the position of her cell. They needed a plan of the interior of the prison. With characteristic energy, she bicycled through the paved streets of Bayonne searching among the cafés for someone who could get inside the prison and obtain a plan of it. She knew many smugglers and black-market operators who frequented these *bistros*. Smugglers were invaluable helpers of her escape organisation. They were able to obtain things in Spain which were no longer available and to sell in Spain what no one could afford to buy in France. Such men at first avoided her, but once their confidence had been gained, she was able to make good use of them. They were daring enough to undertake dangerous assignments. During the years in which she presided over the southern part of the Comet route, they worked for her loyally.

The man she chose for the task of reconnoitring the prison was a plumber, with a round, red face which earned him the nickname 'Moon'. In return for a quantity of black-market food, he cheerfully undertook the task of entering the prison.

The official plumber of the prison was a cousin of Jean

Dassié. Jean had agreed to arrange that his cousin should declare himself ill and unfit for work. 'Moon' would then replace him in the prison. 'Moon' was to study the interior and obtain all possible information about Dédée and her cell and whether a rescue attempt was feasible. After voluble deliberations, cut short by the commanding Tante Go, the cousin agreed to report sick. 'Moon' then offered his services to the prison authorities and presented himself for work.

But on the morning of his arrival he was met by shattering news. Dédée had been transferred the evening before to Fort du Hâ in Bordeaux. She was again in the hands of the Gestapo.

The airmen with whom Dédée had been arrested at Urrugne had been harshly interrogated. One of them, overcome by threats and blows, had described to the Gestapo the route which the ill-fated party of 13 January had followed from Bayonne to Francia's farm. He had accompanied officers of the Gestapo through the streets of Bayonne and revealed the house in which he had been hidden. The effect of this was to lead his interrogators to think that the headquarters of the Comet Line was in the south of France, perhaps in Bordeaux. Dédée, when questioned, did nothing to undeceive them. She was not, therefore, detained at Fort du Hâ. She was sent back to the Villa Chagrin. Her real identity was still not known to the Germans.

'Moon', prospecting next morning in the office of the Governor of the prison, observed the list of prisoners and the numbers of their cells. He was able to confirm the joyful news to Tante Go, Franco and 'B' Johnson that Dédée was back. The rescue plan could proceed.

Next day 'Moon' contrived to visit Dede's cell. The figure of a woman lay on the bed. At first glance 'Moon' was astonished to see she had grey hair. And then, looking at her as closely as he dared in the presence of the *gardien*, he saw that she was young. He did not know then that Dédée had dyed her hair black and that its own lighter tint was beginning to reappear.

'Moon' tinkered vaguely with the stove in the cell and studied the chances of escape. His eyes lighted on the ventilator in the wall. Under the watchful surveillance of the *gardien*, he examined it as closely as he could. It was large enough, if it could be forced, for Dédée's agile body to pass through. But it would need several visits to the cell to loosen it from the wall. He reported back to Tante Go.

'Get into the cell as often as you can under any pretext. Sing out a few phrases in Spanish. She understands,' said Tante Go.

'What shall I say?'

'I will give you your orders when the ventilator is forced,' retorted Tante Go.

There was little time. Next morning 'Moon' saw a new list of prisoners, and against the number of the Cyclone's cell was written what he took to be the name 'De Tonga'. Whatever the explanation for this curious spelling of De Jongh, it was evident that the Gestapo were hot on the track of the Cyclone.

Within twenty-four hours, Tante Go had made new plans. If Dédée could get through the ventilator, she could drop to the roof of a one-storey building below her cell.

Here, active as she was, she could easily drop into the courtyard. 3 February, the day chosen for her escape, was one on which, at the changing of the guard, there would be only three German soldiers in the prison. On that night two of them had accepted invitations to drink wine with Fernand De Greef,

Tante Go's husband, and the faithful Jean Dassié. Tante Go was confident that at the hour chosen for the attempt they would be drunk in the Bar Gachy.

She gave her orders of the day. At nine o'clock in the evening, Franco and 'B' Johnson, dressed in the stolen uniforms of German officers, would ring at the gates of the prison and demand entrance. It was hoped that the remaining German, realising that his comrades were absent from duty without permission, would be scared and allow Franco and 'B' to enter the prison. They would detain the German in conversation while Dédée, having escaped through the ventilator, hid in the shadows of the courtyard. At a favourable moment, Dédée would make a dash through the gates.

On the morning of 3 February, 'Moon' was singing gaily in Spanish outside the door of Dédée's cell. One phrase that he chanted included the word 'tomorrow', but she replied:

'No, Sunday.'

Sunday was the next day, and the conspirators were in confusion. For Tante Go, unlike Dédée, knew that the Germans had by now discovered her identity. 'Moon' was ordered back to the prison and told to contact Dédée somehow. He was prepared to take every risk, to file away a portion of the ventilator on that very day. It must open easily and without delay. The *gardien* unlocked the door for him with his jangling keys. The cell was empty. The mattress was rolled up and, turning to the door, 'Moon' saw that the name 'De Tonga' had been removed. He returned to the Bar Gachy with the news that Dédée had been once more taken away, and this time, it appeared, permanently.

It was a bitter disappointment, but Tante Go never gave in.

She ordered her supporters to find out Dédée's new prison and, if possible, to plan a new escape. Within a few hours her spies had discovered that Dédée was at the prison known as Maison Blanche at Biarritz. Next morning Tante Go with 'B' Johnson watched from a house overlooking the prison, which belonged to a friend of Jean Dassié. From the second storey of this house they could see Dédée's slim figure walking at exercise in the courtyard. The prison, like the Villa Chagrin, was small and not well guarded. One flash of sunlight from a pocket mirror, directed to the courtyard, attracted the prisoner's attention. She knew that her friends had followed her.

Tante Go discovered that Madame 'X', the Red Cross prison visitor, also saw the prisoners of Maison Blanche, and would therefore be able to contact Dédée. For the second time she sought the Frenchwoman's help. But Madame 'X' was afraid. A look of horror came into her eyes as she told the forceful, impatient Tante Go:

'If the Gestapo interrogate me, I do not know what I shall say.'

This woman could be dangerous, thought Tante Go.

'If we can rescue Dédée, then we must kidnap her too. She may be a patriot, but she is too frightened.'

They made their plans to abduct this timid creature.

For the next week Tante Go and Jean Dassié continued their preparations. By now the countryside was filled with rumours about the imprisoned Cyclone and the attempts to deliver her from the enemy. Jean Dassié exposed himself to every danger by telephoning urgent messages through the exchange at Bayonne. Suddenly came the news which made their hearts beat faster. The airman from whom the Gestapo had forced some information had given further details of the people who had hidden

ABOVE Andrée De Jongh (Dédée), known by her father as 'the Little Cyclone'.

LEFT Andrée De Jongh's fake identity card as Denise Lacroix.

Frédéric De Jongh (Paul), who was already working with the resistance when his daughter set up the Comet Line and then controlled it from Brussels until his arrest in 1942. He was executed by firing squad in Paris in March 1944.

Andrée De Jongh's mother, Alice.

Suzanne Wittek, Andrée De Jongh's sister and one of the members of the Comet Line.

Airey Neave, who joined MI9 in 1942 after escaping from Colditz.

Baron Jean Greindl (Nemo), who ran the Comet Line under cover of his work for the Red Cross from mid-1942 until his arrest in the summer of 1943.

The Red Cross card of Peggy van Lier, who was the chief assistant to Baron Jean Greindl (Nemo).

Victor Michiels (Louis), one of the 156 members of the Comet Line who were killed by the Germans. He died on 19 November 1942, aged 26.

The Hanotte family, who smuggled escapers over the border between Belgium and France. Henriette Hanotte (Monique), seen kneeling, was also a guide on the route from the Belgian border to Paris.

The Villa Voisin in Anglet, south-west France, where Elvire De Greef (Tante Go) and her family hid escapers before they were smuggled across the Pyrenees to Spain and freedom.

The De Greef family, who ran the Villa Voisin safe house. Elvire De Greef (front left) is holding her dog Gogo, from whom she took her codename, Tante Go.

Lily Dumont (Michou) hid escapers
in Brussels and Paris and also acted as
a guide between Paris and the Pyrenees.

Elsie Mary 'Polly' Maréchal, an
Englishwoman married to a Belgian,
and one of the members of the Comet
Line incarcerated in Ravensbrück
concentration camp. She survived.

Elsie Maréchal, daughter of 'Polly', and a
Comet Line guide. She was incarcerated
with her mother in Ravensbrück and
several other camps. She survived.

Georges Maréchal, who had spent the
First World War in Britain and married
an Englishwoman. He was one of the
members of the Comet Line shot by
the Germans in October 1943.

Albert 'B' Johnson, the Englishman who helped the De Greef family hide escapers in Anglet, with his wife Wendy.

The identity card of Georges d'Oultremont, who was a guide on the route from Belgium to Paris.

Andrée De Jongh with a clock from an RAF bomber presented to her after the war.

Jean-François Nothomb (Franco), Andrée De Jongh's lieutenant on the run from Paris to the Pyrenees and, following her arrest, the head of the Comet Line. The British officer (right) is Major Richard Brinsley Ford of MI9.

Francia's farm and Comet Line safe house at Urrugne in south-west France, where Andrée De Jongh was arrested on 15 January 1943. She and the owner of the house, Francia Usandizanga, were taken to Ravensbrück. De Jongh survived but Usandizanga died there on 12 April 1945, aged 36.

Andrée De Jongh (Dédée), Lily Dumont (Michou) and Elvire De Greef (Tante Go) with Airey Neave in London after the war. All three were awarded the George Medal.

Andrée De Jongh celebrating her 90th birthday.

Soldiers from the Belgian Military Academy taking the same route over the Bidassoa river used by the escapers, to commemorate the work of the Comet Line.

them in Bayonne. Among them Jean Dassié and his wife and Monsieur and Madame Lapeyre, two loyal members of Tante Go's organisation.

So early one morning the Gestapo came for Jean Dassié. In the living room of his little house they studied the decorations for gallantry he had won in the First World War. They stood before the frames in which they hung on the wall and saluted with heavy irony. Then they led away Jean and his wife. They took with them also his daughter of sixteen. Only their little son of seven remained alone in the house.

Tante Go, with her sharp instinct for danger, cycled round Bayonne, warning her helpers, and thus succeeded in saving the family Lapeyre before the Gestapo arrived at their house. Her husband, Fernand De Greef, and her son, Freddy, snatching every morsel of news from the *Kommandantur* at Anglet, informed her that the Gestapo was ready to make more arrests. From her cell at Maison Blanche, Dédée sent this pitiful message:

'*Les enfants ont parlé.*'

Dédée and Jean Dassié were taken by the Gestapo to confront the airmen. It was a painful and embarrassing moment. For Jean Dassié, who had housed these men, the situation was hopeless, but he refused to make one single admission. As for his wife and sixteen-year-old daughter, they too withstood all threats and blows. For Madame Dassié, thinking of her boy of seven alone at home, the temptation to confess was terrible. And yet she revealed nothing. Father, mother and daughter were deported to Germany to suffer torture and privation. And in the hour of liberation, Jean Dassié returned to France. He lived for a few days, a tragic shell of a man, and died as he was reunited with his gallant family in Paris. Such was the story of this splendid Frenchman.

By the middle of February, the Gestapo appeared to be satisfied, for they stopped their inquiries in Bayonne. Tante Go and her family breathed again. It had been a hair's breadth escape for them, but they were still ready to try to free the girl who for so long had been the moving spirit of the Line.

But it was too late to save Dédée. The arrest of Jean Dassié had filled many hearts with fear, and Tante Go could not rouse her former colleagues. It was with tears that Franco and Tante Go, from a vantage point at the station at Bayonne, saw the Dassié family and Dédée in handcuffs walk to the train for Paris. Over the window of the compartment the Germans had fixed an iron grille. And as the train left Bayonne the watchers felt that they would never see Dédée and Jean Dassié and his family again.

## Chapter Twelve

## *Cantine Suédoise*

T he arrest of Dédée was a tragedy beyond all telling. In the south the Line was virtually destroyed, and Tante Go had been forced to lie low. In Paris, Paul had returned sadly to the Rue Vaneau, and Nemo was trying to restore the Brussels end of the Line.

Dédée had been a vital flame. She had encouraged her followers and taught them that whatever blows the enemy might strike, the sacrifices were worthwhile. Soon her unquenchable spirit rallied the waverers, who began to forge new links in the broken chain.

The *débâcle* of the *Cantine Suédoise* left Nemo alone with Jean Ingels and Eric de Menten. Over 100 people had been arrested in two days after the murderous visit of the false Americans to Madame Maréchal's house in the Avenue Voltaire. Peggy and Edouard and Georges d'Oultremont had gone to England in December. Nemo knew that he had no longer the strength to carry on. He must find a successor as leader of the Brussels end of the Line.

So, early in January 1943, before Dédée had left on her last journey to Spain, he went to Paris with Jean Ingels and Eric de Menten to see her and her father at the Rue Vaneau. Paul and his daughter had made their headquarters in this dismal street, which adjoins the Rue Oudinot. There they lived, with Franco, in a modern but cheerless block of flats. In spite of the heroic act of Elvire in swallowing the paper with their address at the Rue Oudinot, they had thought it prudent to move. It was in the small living room of this new flat that the three leaders of Comet met and discussed the future.

Nemo had not seen Dédée since her audacious visit to Brussels in May of the previous year. It was then that they had come to know each other's characters. Dédée had been dramatic, impulsive and impatient for action. Nemo had tried to calm her, but they had parted full of admiration for their different qualities.

In January 1943, he had come to Paris to see Dédée and tell her that he could not continue. The Cyclone, after twenty-four crossings of the Pyrenees, looked thinner and less robust, but her determination was undimmed. She would have no weakening at any part of the Line. This resolve was clearly written in her eyes.

Nemo opened the conversation, laying stress on the effect of the November disaster in Brussels. Jean Ingels and Eric de Menten were beside him.

'The British do not understand how difficult it is to persuade our helpers and guides to go on. People have heard of poor Victor's death. They know how many hostages have been taken. Over one hundred people arrested in two days!'

Dédée looked at Nemo. He, too, was thinner, but still calm and elegant.

She spoke with pride in her voice. She had no doubts:

'In London, people are delighted with our work.'

'Perhaps, but they do not understand the risks that we run.'

Dédée frowned.

'That is not the point. We have got to go on, and the reason is this. The numbers of airmen coming back are now so large that they are helping the morale of the aircrews. When a man returns alive and safe he is a living proof to his friends that over here there are people to help them if they, too, are shot down. It gives them heart on their raids.'

Her eloquence delighted the men from Brussels. She spoke with fierce conviction. They were charmed by her smiling determination. Tired as they were and apprehensive of the future, they were roused to action.

If only Dédée and her hearers could have realised to the full the truth of what she said! None of them was ever to see an airman returned home after being given up for lost; to see the effect on his friends of his first appearances in the mess at his station. They had done more than anything else to take the sense of hopelessness out of the sceptical words 'Missing' or 'Missing believed killed'.

When she looked again at Nemo, Dédée knew that she had won. He rose and paced about the dreary sitting room among the yellow, varnished furniture. His face had changed. Its pallor was gone and there was a new, lively expression in his eyes.

'Are you going on?' asked Dédée eagerly.

'Yes, of course. If that is what you say, Dédée, we will continue, whatever the cost. Are you two with me?' He turned to Jean Ingels and Eric de Menten.

They nodded and smiled.

Nemo spoke again:

'Now we have got something to tell people. Now we can say to those who feed and house the airmen that the risks are worthwhile, that our work is appreciated. But I am afraid that things are not too good in Brussels.'

'You must take care of yourself, Nemo,' said Dédée. 'One day you will have to come out. In the meantime do not go near the *Cantine*. Supposing someone has been forced to talk about it.'

Nemo laughed for the first time that fateful evening.

'If things get dangerous, I shall hide. I shall work from a flat which only Jean and Eric shall know about. I shall also look for someone to replace me, and when I have found him, I shall be off to England.'

There was a silence. Nemo, the aristocrat, stood up and faced the schoolmaster's young daughter. His slim, smart figure had acquired new confidence and poise. He shook hands with Dédée and her father and then with a slight bow, with his two friends he turned to the door.

'Do not go near the *Cantine*, Nemo,' said Dédée deliberately.

Nemo smiled and was gone.

'That is a splendid man,' said Paul. 'But I fear that we shall not meet again.'

As he sat with his companions in the train to Brussels, Nemo, too, felt that he had had his last meeting with Dédée and Paul.

In Brussels, Nemo described the meeting to his young wife. The weeks which had followed the terrible disaster of the false Americans had been a stern test for both of them. At the beginning of December, Bernadette, Baronne Jean Greindl, had given birth to their second child. He was a son, born amid turmoil and grief. Nemo saw him only once at this mother-in-law's house in the Rue Froissart. He came there in secret, fearing desperately that he might be followed. His wife turned anxiously to him:

'You are going to stop and escape before it is too late?'

'No, I am going on until I find my successor. Dédée has persuaded me.'

'It is sheer madness.'

Nemo shrugged his shoulders. In a moment he had gone out into the wintry streets. Next day he heard with grief of Dédée's arrest.

At the *Cantine Suédoise*, only Commandant Bidoul remained at his desk, dolefully studying his account books. The meetings in the dusty little office were over. The happy days of Georges and Elsie and Peggy seemed far away. Treachery was at every street corner. Only kindly and erratic Madame Scherlinck remained blissfully ignorant of the drama, for when Nemo spoke to her on the telephone he assured her that all was well.

Nemo went into hiding at his new flat at the Place Blyckaert. Here Jean Ingels and Eric de Menten would visit him. There came also his brother, Albert Greindl, who had helped him in the past and who was fast becoming suspect to the Gestapo. These three would often sit together on a darkening afternoon and speak of Dédée. Nemo's thoughts would go back to the summer morning in 1942 when she had first appeared before him in Brussels. It seemed then that the Line between Brussels and Paris had fallen in ruins after the arrest of Charlie Morelle. Then she had said to him without hesitation:

'You realise that there are nine chances out of ten that you will never come out of this alive?'

Nemo had said nothing: he had simply smiled; and Dédée knew that he had accepted his fate. He would be loyal to the end. He understood the meaning of fear more than she did. She had carefree youth. He was oppressed by anxiety for his wife and his family.

Their second meeting had been at a happy moment when Nemo had brought to Paris three British Army officers, who had escaped from Germany. There had been a cheerful evening of wine and rejoicing in the success of the Line. Then there had been that third dramatic meeting at the Rue Vaneau a few days before her arrest.

Dédée, the schoolmaster's daughter, and Nemo, the Baron, were two of the foremost leaders in the history of underground war. Each fascinated those who worked for them. Resistance became a sacred duty. They had the power to give others the strength to face death and torture.

As January drew to a close, Nemo faced a hard decision. On the one side, his friends implored him to go to England. On the other, there remained the question of his successor as chief of the Line. Who could it be? For the moment he must stay and fight.

A fortnight after the arrest of Dédée, a smuggled message from Paris brought fresh hope. Two parachutists from England were coming to help Nemo rebuild the shattered Line. Nemo was greatly cheered. The Line might be independent, but at least the British were thinking of him and his work. Each night he sat by his radio at Place Blyckaert waiting for a BBC message that signalled their arrival. He had been warned that they would drop near the field of Waterloo, but he dare not go to meet them. He gave orders that they should be hidden until their identity had been established.

The two men dropped on a dark night near the village of Bois-Seigneur-Isaac.[†] The long, white château of the family

---

†     The two parachutists landed on the outskirts of the Bois d'Hautmont (commune d'Ophain – Bois-Seigneur-Isaac). One of them was housed by Mr and Mrs François Bar.

of Snoy lay shuttered and quiet. Through its doors, Nemo and his bride had walked from their wedding one gay spring morning five years before. Many guests had followed them down the long avenue. The high rooms within rang with laughter and there was the flash of decorations. Now, on this dark January night, the old château of Bois-Seigneur-Isaac stood calm and faithful, as it had done over the centuries.

Next day two young Belgians met Nemo at an address which they had been given in England. He studied them politely. They brought with them to identify themselves two small medals of Notre Dame de Hal. Instantly Nemo understood. They were the same as the medals which Peggy had given to members of his team before she left for England. So she had reached there safely! More important was a transmitting set with which he could communicate with England. They had messages, too, these shy Belgian youths, sent by the British. One of them, named Henri, spoke:

'The British have sent us to help and they are delighted with your work. I believe they are going to give you a decoration.'

Nemo had a warm feeling of pleasure. After these long, dangerous months, it was heartening to hear this message from England.

'What else have you brought me?'

'Half a million francs.'

Nemo laughed. 'They are doing us proud, aren't they? Let us have a look at your papers.'

He took the identity cards from the two parachutists and studied them.

'These are obvious forgeries. You will have to go into hiding

for the next few days, until we get you something better. When
can we start using the Wit set?'

Back at the flat in the Place Blyckaert, which he rarely left,
he conferred with Eric de Menten.

'Now perhaps we can get started again. We have communication with England.'

And Eric, young and merry, grinned broadly. He had the
true spirit of the *Cantine Suédoise*. Sometimes came Jean Ingels,
who was, in contrast, serious and thoughtful. His eyes had a
remote, mystic look. Poor Commandant Bidoul was still at the
*Cantine*. Every day Nemo would telephone him:

'*Rien de suspect, Monsieur le Baron,*' assured the Commandant.

At this time there came a letter from Suzanne Wittek,
Dédée's sister, who was still in the prison of St Gilles, written
in a neat, compact hand and smuggled out no one knew how.
Nemo read it carefully. '*Cher c'est atroce*' it began ['c'est atroce'
was her nickname for Nemo]…

Charlie [Morelle] was taken with all the papers on him. He was
tortured at first. Now he is left alone. His morale is magnificent. He has tried twice to escape. He has some chance, but
very little, of saving himself.

As for me, my situation is not too bad. They know all
about the Line to San Sebastián. They have done so for a
long time.

Nadine [Andrée Dumont] has been splendid. She never
admitted anything until they started to beat her mother and
then only so as incriminate herself… Her father hasn't a
chance, but they will release the mother…

Elvire has stood it well. In addition to the paper with the

Paris address which she swallowed, she had a photograph of Dédée, fortunately not very good... Also a parcel with files and a hacksaw, in some cakes, and a letter from Dédée which was meant for Charlie. They think the cakes were provisions for our '*enfants*'! They have not opened them!

We are all in communication. For Madame Maréchal, things are bad. For Monsieur, impossible...

Do not worry about me. I am bearing up in prison even if I have to stay here several months. I hope all is going well and I am thinking of you all. Above all, try not to join us here... S.

20.12.42

Nemo put the letter down. Splendid Suzanne! What courage these women had! They were a wonderful example. He wondered for a moment. Would he show the same firmness? It seemed from her letter that the Germans, even if they were aware of the Line, knew nothing of the *Cantine*. Would it be safe to go there and see Bidoul? Things seemed to be getting in order again. Already he had been able to find new recruits, and Henri and the wireless operator would soon be ready. He would risk another visit. A small, laughing voice said far away: 'Don't go near the *Cantine*, Nemo!'

It was Saturday 6 February 1945, a cold, bright morning. In the Avenue des Arts, Nemo, dressed in a dark overcoat, his Eden hat at a jaunty angle, met his friend, Jean Naus. They laughed together, walked to the *Cantine*, and sat in the office smoking cigarettes.

Jean Naus was a businessman. He had a staunch, solid air about him. For a long time past he had risked his life in the resistance. He had aided Nemo in procuring false papers. Today he sits at his office desk in Brussels. His eyes are grey and frank behind his glasses.

Jean Naus will never forget that morning at the *Cantine*. He had known Nemo under the pseudonym of the 'Last of the Mohicans', a *nom de guerre* with poignancy.

Nemo was cheerful as they talked with Commandant Bidoul.

'I know', he said, 'that if I stay here much longer it will be all up with me. Yet I do not feel the Germans know much about this place. I must stay here until my successor is chosen. I must carry on.'

He looked through the frosted panes of the window to the untidy garden. The sun shone brightly. His thoughts were suddenly of the past few months, of Peggy and Georges and Victor... Jean Naus noticed his long, fine hands tapping the side of the desk. He had great qualities this 'Last of the Mohicans' – a real chief.

They talked for a few minutes – Jean was quiet and confident; Nemo lively but a little brusque, often ironic – and Commandant Bidoul watched them, his round, red face full of trust and admiration.

The door burst open. There had been no sound from outside, only the clatter of plates as the children began their morning meal in the room below the office. Four men armed with automatics stood over them. A loud voice barked:

'German Secret Police! Let no one move.'

Nemo felt fear run through his body, so that he felt desperately sick. His stomach seemed to turn within him. A cold sweat came over his forehead and hands. It was the long-feared moment, yet how piercing and terrible it was! He could see poor Commandant Bidoul, his hands above his head, his red face mottled and his eyes rolling piteously.

Nemo had regained control of himself. He was very pale.

The leader of the Gestapo, in a heavy raincoat, his hat pulled down over his eyes, waved his automatic:

'At last, Nemo, we've got you!'

Nemo dimly saw a small, dark, greasy man at the opposite end of the room. His wicked eyes shone with a pleasure at once cruel and ferocious. Here at last were the Gestapo, no less unpleasant than his worst fears. The gay *insouciance* of the *Cantine* had painted them too kindly. The Line had crumbled. He had stayed too long.

Soon he was quite calm. Two of them came to search him. His pockets were emptied, and on the table lay his watch, his wallet, a folded piece of paper.

'What is this?' the German leader in the raincoat snarled, showing the inevitable gold front tooth. He was a poor actor, overdramatising the part.

It was a letter from Nemo to Paul in Paris printed in block letters. It lay there on the table exposed and incriminating. Nemo looked at it in a kind of helpless fury.

'I am not the author. I was only passing it on.'

'We shall see… We shall see.' The man from the Gestapo folded it twice and placed it in a grey leather pocketbook. A clock struck one.

The cars moved down the Rue Ducale as Nemo, Commandant Bidoul and Jean Naus left the *Cantine* for the last time.

At one o'clock other Gestapo agents came for Bernadette Greindl at the Rue Froissart. They seized her roughly, ignoring the brave protests of the baby's nurse, Mlle Schadron, and drove her to an office at the Rue Charles Legrelle. She waited in a cold, bare room, buoyed with the hope that they wanted to question her about her husband, who was still free. A German beckoned her to a small office, where the prisoners were ordered to give details of their identity.

There she saw Nemo. His worn, courageous figure in the doorway seemed to make her heart stop beating. She fought hard against faintness. Nemo came over to her, ignored the lumbering Germans, and held both her hands tightly. His eyes were smiling. He made a faint movement of his head from side to side. Bernadette understood. Their life together was over. She took a rosary from her pocket and held it up before him. Nemo, still smiling, was seized and pushed away as harsh voices sounded all around her. She stood holding the rosary towards him...

The prisoners from the *Cantine* were hustled to the prison of St Gilles and spent two hours in grim discomfort and darkness. Then they were taken back to the Rue Charles Legrelles. Nemo and Jean Naus were handcuffed, back to back. Chairs were pushed beneath them. Jean Naus was the first to be taken for interrogation. He remembers that there were five Germans seated in a circle. Two of them sat on either side of the prisoner with short cudgels, with which they freely struck him across the face. Two bright lamps shone in his eyes. In that unfriendly room the only furniture was a small, white table and an iron bed. The questions came, raining on him like bullets. Sometimes the interrogators would tire and hand over to others. The room became hot – and one, the small pomaded man with cruel eyes – took off his coat and flung it on the bed. He rubbed his hands in anticipation. Jean Naus experienced less violence than the others. He was able to explain his presence at the *Cantine Suédoise* with conviction. The Gestapo knew little about him, and soon he was back with the others where they waited with pounding hearts, nerving themselves for the moment when all their courage would be needed. It was the turn of Nemo. Soon after he was gone there were savage cries from the room above.

After an hour there was silence, then the sound of footsteps on the stairs. Nemo was framed in the doorway, his face white as a sheet. His mouth and nose were swollen and bleeding but he walked with a firm step. He looked at Jean Naus as if to say: '*Tout s'est bien passé.*'

They were handcuffed together once more. It was half-past four in the morning when they were taken back to St Gilles, where, bruised and exhausted, Nemo fell into a troubled sleep.

The Gestapo found nothing at the *Cantine Suédoise*. After the catastrophe of November, every incriminating document, all money and false identity cards had been hidden in the flat at the Place Blyckaert. The morning after Nemo's arrest, Albert Greindl boldly took a taxi, and leaving it waiting, climbed the stairs to the flat. He let himself in with a spare key and with beating heart hastily collected what he could. As he jumped into the taxi outside, a familiar grey car drew up and from it four Germans emerged and hurried to the entrance. They did not seem to notice Albert, who, with a feeling of dread, ordered the taxi-driver to move away, not daring to look behind him.

The Germans, without removing their hats, stood in the office of the concierge firing brutal questions:

'Who usually came to the flat? What are their names?'

The telephone rang, and in the same instant one of the

Gestapo drew his revolver and placed the barrel against the forehead of the concierge:

'Answer the telephone, and if it is for the Baron tell them that it is safe to come here right away.'

The poor, sweating concierge answered the telephone and heard the cheerful voice of Eric de Menten.

'Yes, *Monsieur*,' he said, trembling, 'it is safe to come. There is no one here.'

Eric was determined to get the papers. He knew nothing of the visit of Albert. The carefree, reckless lieutenant felt he must save what he could. Within half an hour, he was at the door of the flat. The concierge, aware only of a grim man with a revolver behind the curtains in his office, told him that all was clear upstairs. Eric, despite the shock of Nemo's arrest, was enjoying the adventure.

As he opened the door of the flat, they stood waiting for him, smiling unpleasantly.

## Chapter Thirteen

# 'B' Johnson

**'B'** Johnson had been in it from the beginning. At the time of Dunkirk he was in the service of a Belgian nobleman as secretary. Unable to return to England, he threw in his lot with the De Greefs, and they were glad to have him at the villa at Anglet, where he worked assiduously in the garden.

He spoke French with a strong English accent. Despite his beret and forged documents, he remained and looked an Englishman. Yet many were the times he waited with Janine at the station at Bayonne to meet the escapers when they arrived from Paris. He stood beside her, spare and polite, well knowing the risks he ran. At the time of the disaster of Urrugne, he had crossed the frontier seven times.

A week after Nemo's arrest, on 14 February 1943, 'B' Johnson and Franco, guided by Florentino, took a party of American pilots to Spain. In the party was Albert Greindl, brother of Nemo, who had salvaged the incriminating documents from the Place Blyckaert and escaped by the skin of his teeth. He now stood looking towards San Sebastián, wondering what would lay in store for him. In spite of the perils he had faced in Brussels, he returned to Occupied Europe in 1944 to give splendid secret service to the Allies and to survive the tortures of the Gestapo.

'B' and Franco watched the storm sweeping towards them

from the mountains. The party lay around them on the cold, damp turf. Each man had a haversack from which he ate a hasty *tartine*. Soon the rains would be borne on the wind. Franco buttoned his coat against the weather and pulled his beret down over his black hair. He surveyed the group as they rested beneath the shadow of the peaks of the Trois Couronnes. Even in this desolate part of the Pyrenees his handsome, slender figure gave him distinction and power. Against a boulder, unmoved by the dank misery of the dawn, Florentino was drinking wine from his *bota*.

The first raindrops fell and the thunder began to rumble. Florentino rose, and bidding the others follow with a wave of his hand, walked off at a great pace. Soon it became a bright morning. They rested again at noon on a wooded slope. Franco surveyed his party. He felt a strong sense of his responsibility. It was he, Franco, twenty-three years old, who had succeeded the incomparable Dédée. No one had dared to think that one day they might be without her. But Franco had faith in himself. It gave him his quiet self-assurance and a sense of command. To maintain the Line, to bring yet more airmen home, was his vow. He owed it to the memory of Dédée.

For 'B' Johnson too the memory of Dédée was golden. As he watched Franco, he wondered how he would compare with her. 'B' had been used to seeing her, cheerfully setting off on many a hazardous journey. And yet, as he stood there, Franco seemed to possess the same spiritual qualities of leadership. They shone in his vivid brown eyes.

The shadows were lengthening for 'B'. As he looked back towards the peaks of France, he was thoughtful. He had served the Comet route from its earliest days. His personal courage was beyond doubt. But his accent and appearance made him a danger to himself and to the organisation. He was now accompanying Franco to get information from the British. It would not be long before he made his last journey across the frontier.

With stiffened limbs, the men rose to their feet and clambered slowly on, making for the village of Elizondo, on the Spanish side. It had been necessary to take the longer route, as the rains had made the Bidassoa impassable. Florentino bade them farewell at a farmhouse on the road to Pamplona, and Franco and his party crowded into a car driven by a Spaniard who had been well remunerated with *pesetas*. Suddenly there were shouts, and from a wood beside the road sprang two *carabineros*. 'B' Johnson and Albert Greindl leapt from the car and ran into the hills, but Franco and the three airmen were cornered. The Spanish driver, briefed to explain that they were French tourists, jabbered incoherently with his hands above his head.

The rain splashed and danced on the road as Franco and the three airmen miserably left the car. There were harsh cries in Spanish; demands for papers; the atmosphere was threatening and officious. The three airmen looked on helplessly.

The *carabineros* stormed about them for several minutes. While one went off to telephone, the other covered the party with his rifle until, in an hour's time, when they were soaked to the skin, a lorry came to collect them. Franco and his companions sat sadly together as they jolted along the road to Pamplona, where they were hustled from the lorry and imprisoned in the town jail. They spent a terrible night in the evil-smelling prison. Franco was interrogated next day.

'What are you?'

'I am a Canadian.'

'What is your occupation?'

'Airman.'

'You look very dark for a Canadian.'

'I am a French Canadian.'

But Franco won the battle of words. The Spaniards believed him to be a pilot escaping with the others. At this period of the war, the authorities had become used to airmen entering their country illegally. When they were satisfied that their prisoners were Allied servicemen, they usually handed them over to the British Consulate.

Franco's story did not deceive the inmates of the prison. There were a number of Frenchmen who had crossed the frontier without guides. Several were trained pilots, anxious to join the Allied Forces in England. They questioned Franco eagerly. Had he flown the latest types of aircraft? What was the Mosquito like? How many cannon had they? And many other technical questions.

Franco would not answer them. Soon his fellow prisoners grew suspicious, shunning him, believing him to be a traitor. To Franco this was an unpleasant but nevertheless ironical experience. He ignored the dark looks, for he knew that Albert and 'B' Johnson had got away. His patience was soon rewarded. The Frenchmen changed their attitude when, a week later, a big blond Englishman came to collect Franco and the Americans. Franco was glad to breathe the fresh air of the hills as the big black Bentley sped towards Bilbao.

When he reached the British Consulate, he learned with gratitude who had been responsible for his release. 'B' and Albert Greindl, after escaping the *carabineros*, had made their way to San Sebastián to report the news. Then mysterious wheels began to turn.

Franco's miraculous release deeply impressed him, and between the young Belgian and the British there now developed a firm bond of sympathy. He felt that they would do all in their power to protect the workers of the Comet Line. The growing influence of the British in Spain was an inspiring sign.

There was no time to be lost in rebuilding the Line. The great raids had begun. The people of Occupied Europe heard for the first time the sound of hundreds of bombers and, from the spring of 1943, the numbers of airmen to be rescued grew. Soon there were Americans in every group which Franco and Florentino brought to Bilbao.

The success of this resuscitated line depended on maintaining the frontier organisation, and in a safe marshalling point for the airmen in Paris. Already a French girl had been found to aid Franco as a guide from Paris. Her name was Madeleine Bouteloupt. She was thirty and, like many of those who served the Line, had a staid and modest appearance. She had large brown eyes, whose innocence deceived many a *gendarme* and ticket inspector on the route to Bayonne. From the middle of April 1943, she met parties of men from Brussels, at the Gare Montparnasse in Paris.

Madeleine led them, as Dédée had done, through the darkened station where *gendarmes* and Gestapo stood at every barrier. As evening fell she took them to meet Franco on the platform at the Gare d'Austerlitz.

While they were delighted to have found this valuable recruit. Franco and Tante Go were deeply concerned about Paul. They sent 'B' Johnson to Paris to tell him that he must

leave France as soon as the weather improved. But Paul knew
that he would never leave France. While Dédée was imprisoned
on the Continent he would never flee to England. 'B' Johnson
saw that it was useless to try to convince him, and returned by
the night train to Bayonne.

Next morning, as 'B' stepped from the train, he was met by
Tante Go and her friend Madame Lapeyre. Tante Go briskly
proposed an expedition inland from Bayonne to search for a
new route over the frontier. The coastal zone had become too
dangerous. Controls increased daily and there was a multipli-
cation of new passes and certificates. 'B' Johnson had already
collected two addresses in Paris of people who would help in the
frontier region. And thus all three of them boarded a puffing
local train to Ustaritz, ten miles south of Bayonne.

The journey had lasted barely a quarter of an hour when the
train was searched by Germans. To Tante Go and her companions, who had experienced such things time and time again, it
did not seem serious. They expected nothing more than the usual
examination of papers. But the Germans accosted 'B', showing
unwelcome interest in his Anglo-Saxon appearance and accent.

'Where have you come from?' they demanded.

'Paris,' said 'B'.

And he showed his ticket, which he had not given up at
Bayonne. Tante Go showed the tickets which she had bought
at Bayonne for Ustaritz. The Germans were not satisfied. They
began a search for papers. 'B' Johnson had several incriminating
documents and addresses in his pocketbook. It was a dangerous
moment.

'I am going to be sick!' cried Madame Lapeyre. 'Please will
someone open the window?'

She turned to 'B' with a look that he quickly understood. With the permission of the guards, he pulled down the window. As he did so, a handful of papers fluttered from the carriage. The Germans seemed not to have noticed this ruse. They took their three prisoners to a compartment at the rear end of the train, where a temporary office was set up. The interrogation began anew.

Pocketbooks, handbags and tickets were examined again. An officer of the *Feldgendarmerie* asked why they were travelling to Ustaritz. He turned to Tante Go.

'This man is an Englishman, is he not?'

Tante Go looked at the German. Her round eyes expressed a mixture of surprise and scorn.

'No, he is Belgian, but he has an English mother. That is why he has such fair skin. I call him Jonion.'

The officer roared:

'He is an airman who has escaped, and you are taking him over the frontier! We know that women do that! We have caught one recently!'

'Do not be ridiculous,' said Tante Go.

'You be careful what you say, Madame.' He turned to 'B' Johnson. 'This identity card is fake. We know you are an escaped airman.'

'B' was indignant. His voice, raised in anger, sounded more English than ever.

'*Mais non!* I am going to the doctor!'

The Germans would not listen. All three were taken to the frontier town of St Jean Pied de Port. There they found themselves with a number of other suspects in a wooden hut. The door was not locked, and outside a bored sentry paced up and down. One of their fellow prisoners, a young Basque, slowly pushed open the door, and at the moment that the guard was farthest from the hut, he raced off across the frontier road. He was followed by the Germans and their officers, firing wildly with rifles and revolvers. The door was still open.

'Go on, 'B'! Now is your chance,' said Tante Go.

'No, Tante. If I do, it will make things worse for you. It will make them think that I really am an escaped airman. They will interrogate you even more. They will send you to the Gestapo, and we cannot risk that. If we tell a good story now, we may still get out.'

The Germans returned without the Basque. They were furious. Their anger was vented on other prisoners in the hut. The three stalwarts of the Comet Line sat together on a bench. Madame Lapeyre was crying quietly. Tante Go was knitting, as she always did on a journey. As for 'B', his very calmness seemed to Tante Go to be too English. The more she looked at him, the more obviously Anglo-Saxon he was, despite his Belgian papers.

There was another interrogation, and 'B', still the principal suspect, was dragged away by four soldiers. He was taken to the ancient palace of the Princes-Évêques in the town of St Jean Pied de Port. This medieval ruin forms part of the fortifications of the town, and the prison selected for 'B' Johnson was a deep, dark *oubliette*. He lay there in the damp throughout the night. He was chilled to the bone. When dawn came at last, he was too cold to speak.

Meanwhile, as darkness fell at the frontier post, Tante Go loudly demanded of the Germans what they intended to do with her. Then she threatened to report them to the *Kreis Kommandant* of Biarritz.

'I am sure that he would be sorry to hear that you have arrested me.'

'Do you know him?' asked an officer of the *Feldgendarmerie*.

'I know a lot about him.'

'We do not believe you,' roared her inquisitor. There was a faint apprehension in his voice.

'Then ring him up and find out!' cried Tante Go.

The Germans hesitated. They began to ask more questions about 'B' Johnson. But Tante Go would not be diverted. She explained that certain addresses found on 'B' were those of persons ready to supply the *Kommandant* with black-market produce. It was her task, she said, to buy hams, butter, chocolate and eggs on his behalf. As for 'B', he was a young man she had befriended. He suffered from tuberculosis, and she was taking him to the doctor in Ustaritz.

The Germans, always submissive at the mere mention of superior officers, listened attentively.

'The young man has lived at my house. You can see by his identity card. The doctor thought he was ill, so he was sent to Paris. But they could not do anything for him.'

'Why does he come to Ustaritz?'

'Because there is a sanatorium,' said Tante Go brightly. 'You see, my husband does not wish him to stay in our house. My friend Madame Lapeyre suggested the sanatorium, and we were bringing him here.'

Tante Go began to fear she had overplayed her hand. She turned from this romanesque story to the black market. It aroused less suspicion, and it was a subject which she understood well.

'By all means go and check up on this address and see

whether you can get anything on the black market there,' said Tante Go, confidentially.

Since everyone she knew in the resistance movement had at some time been engaged in the black market, Tante Go had little fear that the Germans would be disappointed. In an hour's time two Germans returned laden with food. One of them grabbed a piece of chocolate. The remainder greedily surveyed the rare delicacies.

Tante Go stared at them. They were embarrassed. 'Those provisions belong to me,' she said sternly. 'It is my duty to take them to the *Kreis Kommandant*. He will pay me.'

The Germans looked sheepishly at the food.

Tante Go shouted at them.

'If you touch it I shall complain to the *Kommandantur*. My husband works as interpreter for the *Kommandant* at Anglet. If you do not let me go he will make inquiries for me. There will be a terrible row about this black-market food.'

The Germans, frightened of exposure, were undecided. One of them – a large, red-faced individual – said:

'Well, perhaps she had better take the food.'

'But what are you going to do with the poor young man you have taken to your prison?' cried Tante Go.

She was really alarming in her passion.

'I do not care about this food. Let the young man go.' And the Germans, seeking a solution from this predicament, released her and Madame Lapeyre. They took the two women to an hotel, escorting them nervously through the streets with a dark lantern. At the door of the hotel Tante Go said:

'What are you going to do about the young man?'

'He will be released tomorrow. He will be put on the train, and you can meet him there.'

The promise was kept. 'B' Johnson was on the train next morning. Tante Go explained to him that he had been exchanged for a hamper of black-market food.

'I thought I was worth more than that!' he said with indignation.

'B's time had come. On 13 March 1943, he said goodbye. He crossed the frontier with Franco for the last time, accompanied by Monsieur and Madame Lapeyre, still searched for by the Gestapo.

## Chapter Fourteen

# Jean Masson

Paul lived on at the Rue Vaneau in Paris through the spring of 1943 under the name of Monsieur Moreau. Often he was seen walking in the streets, an indomitable bowed figure, with eyes that smiled in kindly fashion behind horn-rimmed spectacles. In the month of May he was again taking men across Paris from station to station for the journey south. His grief at the arrest of Dédée and Suzanne Wittek aroused in him a reckless activity. He had abandoned all thought of escape to England. His tortured mind dwelt only on the fate of his family. For their sake he desired passionately to carry on the Line.

In such circumstances his presence in Paris was a risk not only to himself but also to others. There were those who implored him to leave. They warned him that his arrest might mean the death of his daughter. He was, indeed, in constant peril. His frequent appearances at railway stations with airmen were wildly imprudent. Of this he was only dimly aware. He had lost all sense of his own safety. He wanted only to be near her.

He was convinced that the Cyclone was in mortal danger. He sought by every means to save her life. Franco, on his visits to Bilbao, brought messages from him imploring the British to intercede for her with a neutral Power or to exchange her for a captured German agent. Like the family of Nemo, he strove to acquaint influential friends of her plight. His actions were dangerous in the extreme. At the end of March he crossed the frontier into Switzerland trying to gain support for a *démarche* to the Germans. The British, cautious as ever, feared the result of such operations. They preferred to do nothing. It was safer.

For weeks after the arrest of Dédée, the Line had been at a standstill, broken only by the energy and courage of Franco and Tante Go. The 'safe' houses in Paris were full to overflowing, and there was grave risk of detection. Paul worked hard to find an outlet. He made contact with other organisations in France and handed over to them some of the waiting airmen.

In April he had acquired a new guide for the route from Brussels to Paris. His name was Jean Masson, a Belgian, who had for some months past worked for the resistance in northern France. He had thus become acquainted with genial Robert Aylé. To Robert, Jean Masson proposed his services as guide, and Robert, anxious to help the schoolmaster from Belgium, presented his new friend at the Rue Vaneau.

Jean Masson came from Tourcoing, on the frontier of Belgium and France. He was small of stature, with untidy blond hair. He was, perhaps, twenty-five. Only his fierce eyes made him unusual. The sort of man, thought Paul, who would do well as a guide. He would not easily be noticed in a crowd of passengers. Officials at a frontier control post or at the exit of a big station would not pay him particular attention.

For Paul was anxious about the crossing of the Belgian frontier, which was now more strongly controlled than ever. It had become virtually impossible for someone who did not speak French to get past the *douaniers* at Quiévrain and Blanc-Misseron. The old tricks employed by Dédée and Elvire would no longer avail. He discussed these obstacles with Jean Masson.

The young man was polite and helpful. He spoke of the problem reassuringly, and Paul was impressed by his resourcefulness.

'I can help you, Monsieur Moreau.'

'How?'

'I have a friend who has obtained a quantity of blank passes for the frontier. These are the type which Belgian workmen use every day to cross to France. We can get as many as we like. Have a look, *Monsieur*.'

Paul took the sheaf of forms. There was no doubt of their usefulness.

'What about stamping them?'

'No trouble at all. Here is the stamp. I had it copied to help someone through the other day.'

It was a stamp of the *Feldgendarmerie* for the Lille region.

'This would mean crossing into the Lille district?'

'Yes, you see I come from Tourcoing. I have contacts there. I am afraid there is nothing to be done about Quiévrain. That is hopeless.'

'How many men could you get through at a time with these worker's passes?'

'Oh, ten at least.'

Jean Masson seemed smooth and competent. As he spoke, he looked at Paul. There was a steadfastness about him which appealed to the schoolmaster.

'But I suppose there is a register of these workmen who are allowed to pass? Surely there is some check?'

'Oh, yes. There is a list which the *douaniers* check, but the workmen often go through in groups. All they need is for one of them to hand in a list, and the others hold out their passes, which are seldom examined.'

'But the names on your list are false?'

'So are the names which my friend has provided for the *douaniers*!'

Paul laughed happily. He seemed a splendid man, this disarming Jean Masson! The information from others who knew him was encouraging. The friends of Robert in the resistance had reported him to be reliable, punctual, discreet…

'What do you think?' said Paul as he sat with Robert in the book-lined flat on the top floor of No. 37 Rue de Babylone. Germain poured coffee for them. They could look out over Paris and see the red, white and black of the flags of Nazi Germany waving from public buildings. It was Hitler's birthday.

'I think we should try him.'

And so, on 15 May 1943, Jean Masson was sent to Brussels to collect airmen and bring them to the Gare Montparnesse and then pass them to Madeleine Bouteloupt for Franco to take to Spain. He arrived a few days later with seven men. Franco was still in the south, but Madeleine, Robert and Paul, who met them, were full of praise for the new guide.

'Well done, young man!' exclaimed Paul the schoolmaster. 'Will you continue working for us as guide between Brussels and Paris?'

'Certainly, Monsieur Moreau.'

And Jean Masson was enrolled in the organisation.

He seemed quietly absorbed in his task. Paul and Robert Aylé saw him rarely. When he came to the Rue Vaneau he was polite, anxious to please and full of suggestions for improving the Line. Towards Paul he employed an attitude of deference, as befitted a newcomer.

In the first days of June, Jean Masson called on Paul at the

Rue Vaneau. He had changed. He was agitated and pale. His strange eyes were apprehensive.

'Be ready for June 7th. I have a large party from Brussels. You will need all your helpers to take them over on arrival in Paris.'

His tone, thought Paul, was a little peremptory, as if he were giving the orders.

Paul confided in Robert as they discussed their plans.

'He spoke to me as if he were chief, but perhaps it was only nerves.' He sighed. 'If only Dédée were here…'

Robert saw the remote, sad look in his eyes. How long would he last?

But Paul, always trusting and ready to believe the best of his friends, decided that Jean Masson's manner was prompted by enthusiasm. He brushed aside his faint annoyance, and eagerly started to prepare for the party from Brussels.

The first problem to be settled was where to hide the men? There were already forty in different parts of Paris at this time. New lodgings had to be found and new sources of supplies of food and clothing. All was bustle and anticipation. Madeleine Bouteloupt and Raymonde, the girl who went each morning to the Boulevard Raspail to buy provisions for the hidden airmen, were sent to Lille, with instructions to meet Jean Masson and his convoy. Paul and Robert, and his wife, Germaine, were to be waiting for him on the platform of the Gare du Nord at half-past four on the afternoon of 7 June.

When Madeleine Bouteloupt and Raymonde arrived at Lille, Jean Masson was at the station, punctual and precise. To each girl he entrusted an airman. With him were other aircrew dressed in their borrowed clothes, trying vainly to appear inconspicuous. Jean Masson shepherded them to a waiting room without concern.

They had three-quarters of an hour to wait for the train to Paris. Raymonde, separating from the group with her airman, left the station and crossed the street to a little café. She sat with her companion on its terrace watching the people of Lille as they strolled in the sun.

A hand was on her shoulder. A circle of big men was round the table.

She rose, her heart beating wildly. The airman, comprehending, raised his arms above his head as one of the Gestapo drew a gun…

'She has missed the train,' thought Madeleine Bouteloupt.

She sat in the carriage beside her charge, a small Cockney air gunner. Her soft, brown eyes quietly studied the passing countryside. She could hear voices in the corridor and the sliding back of doors. She motioned to the airman, taking her identity card from her handbag and held it ready before her. The door was flung back and two men in civilian clothes stood there.

'Papers!'

Madeleine had done this so often. She stared politely, her handbag open on her lap.

'Madeleine Bouteloupt.' The man spoke slowly and looked at his companion. He put the identity card in his pocket.

'But… ' said Madeleine, her heart beating faster.

'Come with me. German Secret Police!'

She was led to a compartment at the far end of the train. A blonde woman with murderous eyes searched her and struck her across the face. As she was taken from the train, she saw the little Englishman handcuffed, walking disconsolately beside the Gestapo...

Paul had been writing in the *appartement* at the Rue Vaneau as the clock struck four. Beside him was a pile of blank identity cards and *certificats de domicile*. He pushed them to one side and laid down his pen. It was time to hurry to the Gare du Nord. He put on his beret, leaving his raincoat behind, for the afternoon was fine and warm. He did not even trouble to lock away the cards he had so laboriously filled in. After all, he would soon be back. He went by Metro to the Gare du Nord.

Robert and Germaine Aylé were waiting on the platform. They greeted each other happily. They were delighted at the renewed success of the Line.

'Quite like the old days, when Dédée was with us,' whispered Robert.

There was a movement on the platform, and Jean Masson, followed by a number of rather obvious Englishmen and Americans, came towards them. He was smiling broadly and his manner was effusive. They all shook hands and Jean Masson said:

'We had a good journey, and here we are.'

Paul stiffened. He had seen two *gendarmes* suddenly appear from a waiting room. Then came others, until there were twelve at least around them. There was no way out. They were handcuffed and roughly pushed towards the headquarters of the railway police on the station. They sat there on benches, a pitiful band. Beside them were Jean Masson and his bewildered airmen.

Paul's thoughts went back to that night five months ago when the Cyclone had been arrested. But for the downpour in the mountains he would have got away. He would have been in England, safe from the horrors which awaited him. Yet even in that unfriendly room, where *gendarmes* watched his every movement, he was glad that he had stayed.

There had been many an opportunity since January to lock the door of the flat in the Rue Vaneau for the last time and take the train to Bayonne. They had all tried to persuade him to go, but he would not leave that quiet quarter where the Rue Vaneau, the Rue Oudinot and the Rue de Babylone meet. As Monsieur Moreau he had been happy and among new friends. Most of all he could not bring himself to leave Paris while the Cyclone was still at Fresnes. And now, though fear shook his frail body, he felt a growing sense of pleasure that in prison he would be closer to her.

There were curt orders from a man in plain clothes. Paul, holding his handcuffed hands before him, walked out of the station to a waiting car. A smile passed over his worn face. He felt with his arms stretched out and hands clasped, as if he were holding a plate, like Oliver Twist. There was a tremendous shouting and banging of doors. Robert and Paul were together in the back seat of a Gestapo car. Robert looked anxiously for Germaine, until he saw her calmly getting into another car. Of Jean Masson there was no sign.

An hour later the three of them – Paul, Robert and Germaine – were reunited in the office of the Gestapo at the Rue des Saussaies. They sat despondently on benches waiting to be interrogated. Paul's mind was working furiously. Was Franco safe? What had happened to Madeleine and Raymonde? Then he thought of the false identity cards carelessly left on the table at the Rue Vaneau... Oh God! He sighed heavily, and grey-haired Germaine looked at him and tried to smile.

There were steps outside, and they braced themselves to meet their ordeal, but it was Jean Masson. He stood at the door, smiling. There were no handcuffs on his wrists, as there had been at the Metro.

'Jean!' exclaimed Robert eagerly.

Jean Masson spat on the floor in front of them. Then he came closer.

'Well, you fools!' he sneered.

His face was the most unpleasant any of them had ever seen. It was exultant, repellent in its triumph.

Robert was the first to understand and speak:

'You filthy bastard!'

Jean Masson laughed. He minced across the room in a kind of ecstasy, and disappeared. From that moment, Paul, Robert and Germaine vowed that they would suffer all things, even to the last extremity, rather than admit one single fact which would aid the work of the traitor.

The door opened once more, and Paul was pushed violently forward. A German soldier caught him by the collar and forced him up dark steps to an office where three grim figures at a desk awaited him. A leather-thonged whip hung from the wall…

Eight days later Franco returned from Spain and opened the door of the flat at the Rue Vaneau with his own latchkey. He saw scattered identity cards on the table and the pen laid aside. At first he thought that Paul had just left. The window was still open and the curtains fluttered in the breeze. He changed his clothes and searched everywhere for a favourite tie he could not find.

He went into the tiny kitchen to prepare a meal after his long journey. There was a saucepan on the stove. He lifted the lid and saw the vegetables covered with a light mildew. He looked in the cupboard and found the rotting fruit. And Franco, suddenly aware of the awful truth, stuffed the false papers and all the money he could find into a suitcase and hurried down the stairs.

He spent the night at the home of a friend of Charlie Morelle, a certain Max. Next morning they undertook the rashest of all expeditions to get news. At No. 37 Rue de Babylone, the home of the Aylés, there was an ominous quiet. They turned at the top of the long staircase to see on the door of the flat the seals of the Gestapo. At the Rue Oudinot the white-faced concierge could only mutter:

'*La Gestapo est déjà venue.*'

At the flat of Aimable Fouquerel, the cheerful *masseur*, the door, too, was sealed, as if death lay within. The two men went to the Rue Vaneau, grief-stricken and indifferent to danger. They ascended in the lift, which in wartime stopped only at the fifth floor, to save electricity. As Franco stepped out of it, he could hear voices on the landing of the fourth floor, where Paul had lived. A door banged and there was a shuffling of foot and subdued talking. Then, more loudly, he could hear a curt command in German. It was the Gestapo.

With Max, he stood motionless, not daring to move, wait-ing for the Germans to come upstairs to take the lift. At that moment Franco repented of his reckless visit to the Rue Vaneau. With beating heart, he heard footsteps descending the stairs. After an interval, he left the building with Max, thankful at his escape.

And yet, such was Franco's determination to help his old chief and save what could be saved, that he returned the same evening. He removed the seals from the door and searched the secret hiding places of the flat for money and papers. Hiding a number of identity cards, he took the papers away to safety. This time, the Gestapo themselves had been too late.

## Chapter Fifteen

# Casernes d'Etterbeek

In June 1943, Dédée and Nemo met for the last time. Dédée had been moved from Fresnes, and both appeared as witnesses at the trial of one of their helpers in Brussels. In the waiting room of the Palace Hotel, Dédée was able to pass to Nemo touching and courageous messages from his friends, which she had learned by heart.

She saw him only for a brief moment. But Nemo heard her words of loyalty and affection under cover of some banal conversation untill the guards shouted for silence. He smiled warmly at her under the stony eyes of the Germans. He was thin and pale, but there was laughter in his eyes, as there had been in the old days.

Dédée turned to look at him as she was led through the high double doors into the salon where the Luftwaffe court martial awaited her. The months of imprisonment and torture had aged him, but she was filled with admiration for his courage.

These two great leaders knew each other well. Dédée possessed an indifference to fear, an eagerness to do battle which marked her wonderful career. She scoffed at indecision, and she was imbued with an ideal of service to others. She did not fear men nor the pain which they could inflict upon her. The grief which she felt was for those who followed her and suffered in her cause.

In Nemo she found a more tranquil spirit. He had a greater sense of danger, but once he had decided to remain at his post, he faced the consequences serenely.

Dédée marvelled at her own good fortune. The Germans, despite a mass of evidence obtained by brutal methods from less interesting captives, had still failed to grasp the truth. They imagined her to be no more than a guide working under the orders of Paul and Nemo. That so young a girl could be the architect of this bold underground conspiracy did not dawn on the police of the Luftwaffe or the Gestapo.

Dédée was therefore confident that she could withstand interrogation. But for her father and Nemo, her heart was heavy. For Eric de Menten de Hornes, Albert Mélot, Commandant Bidoul, Jean Ingels and Monsieur Maréchal, there was little hope. What fate awaited these companions of that merry company of the *Cantine Suédoise*?

Nemo and his friends had been condemned to death in April. All that long summer they lay in prison while attempts were made to gain mercy from the Germans. The family of Nemo obtained the support of Marshal Mannerheim of Finland.

Months passed in anxious waiting for news, and hopes of reprieve rose and fell. For Nemo's wife the summer provided a long-drawn torture of suspense. In June she was allowed to see him every three weeks in Brussels. He was brought blindfolded to see her at the Gestapo office in the Avenue de l'Yser. He spoke to her for a few minutes under strict guard. He was able to convey to her that he was in a barracks where horses were stabled, but its whereabouts he could not tell. It was only after many secret enquiries that his family discovered that this prison was the *Caserne d'Artillerie* at

Etterbeek, where Belgian *gendarmes* and German artillery were stationed.

The negotiations with the Germans began to fail. There was an unconfirmed story of his reprieve, and then in August came ominous letters from old Marshal Mannerheim. The fate of his followers awaited that of their chief. In St Gilles, each day that passed without news gave them hope. They saw virtue in delay, for none of them had fully realised how their own indifference to personal safety had brought disaster. They had lived those tremendous months of the *Cantine Suédoise* in a dream. They had given little thought to the cruelty and ruthlessness of the forces which opposed them.

After Nemo was condemned to death by the court martial of the Luftwaffe in Brussels he was treated as a prisoner of great importance. He was never kept for more than twenty-four hours in the same cell, but the interrogations and beatings of the first few weeks after his arrest had ceased. His removal to the barracks at d'Etterbeek took place in May. It was an act contrary to international law, for it was a target of significance to Allied bombers.

His room was above the stables, and through a crack in the boarded window of his cell he could see the fading light of evening. It was September now, and he knew every familiar sound in the great barracks. The horses of the German gunners stirred below, and the sound of their hooves was comforting. In the growing darkness he could see a photograph of his wife and family on the bare wall of the room. He watched it in the shadows until he was left alone with his thoughts.

He dreamed that he was back in the Congo on his coffee plantation. It had taken five years to make it from the jungle of bushes on the bank of a stream called Kamami. He had watched the coffee plants grow and his estate prosper.

This scene of his achievement had been charming. There were sweet-scented avenues of hibiscus and bougainvillaea. A rose-brick house had risen among the yellow lilac trees with furniture of mugula wood – the oak tree of the Congo.

The sentry paced outside the cell, and his jackboots sounded on the boards of the passage, rousing Nemo from his reverie. The night was still, and German voices below had died away. Nemo thought of that first meeting with Dédée... He could hear her say again:

'There are nine chances out of ten that you will never come out of this alive.'

'I know.'

But it had been worthwhile.

He could see her walking rapidly away from the *Cantine Suédoise*, her hair blowing in the breeze.

On the morrow, 7 September 1943, the sky was clear. From their different stations in England, bombers and fighters of the Allied Forces took off on that glorious morning. At the Château of Bois-Seigneur-Isaac, fifteen miles from Brussels, the Baron Jean-Charles Snoy, brother-in-law of Nemo, and his family watched them as they flew towards the capital. It was nine-thirty as they heard anti-aircraft fire and heavy detonations. Everywhere in Belgium people were stirred by this tremendous manifestation of Allied power. Workers in the fields waved a welcome.

In his cell, Nemo could hear the throbbing of the engines and the whistle of a bomb as it grew nearer. He felt no fear, only a sense of elation.

From a casement window at Bois-Seigneur-Isaac, his daughter, Claire, aged five, cried suddenly:

'Don't let them bomb Papa!'

A single bomb fell on the barracks of Etterbeek. It pierced the roof of the stables, bursting on the floor of Nemo's cell. Bernadette Greindl, hurrying to the barracks from Bois-Seigneur-Isaac, could see with difficulty through the dust still hanging in the air. There was a mass of broken masonry and splintered wood, but she did not know in what part of the building her husband was imprisoned.

For a terrible day and night there was no news, and then a curt, unexplained message from the Gestapo that Nemo was dead.

Jean-Charles Snoy and the father of Nemo, Baron Paul Greindl, sought by every means to get more news. Two days after the bombardment, Jean-Charles Snoy reached a block of flats from which it was possible to look down on the barracks, and, standing on the roof, he could see the mountain of bricks and plaster and shattered glass. It was obvious that the Germans had done nothing to clear the debris or uncover the bodies.

On 10 September, Nemo's father was informed that he might go next day with a doctor to search for the body. He was in failing health, and Jean-Charles Snoy begged to be allowed to accompany him on this grim journey. At the last moment permission was granted by Obert von Harbon, Chief of Staff to von Falkenhausen, and he was driven by the Town Major, von Sandersleben, to the barracks.

It was nearly eleven o'clock when he arrived, and the digging had already continued for three hours. It was a scene which Snoy will remember all his life. The soldiers straining to remove the mass of rubble in the sunlight; the correct German officers standing in the ruins; and the old father, upright and military, waiting bravely for the corpse of his son.

Soon there was the odour of corruption, and slowly, with great difficulty, the broken roof beams were lifted from the body.

Nemo was lying on his side, with his arms before him, the palms of his hands touching. The expression on his face was peaceful. It was evident that he had died instantly and suffered no pain. The body was filled with splinters, as if the bomb had burst at his feet...

Permission was granted for the body to be removed for burial, on condition that the ceremony was in secret. There were to be no demonstrations and, above all, no flag was to drape the coffin.

On 12 September, Snoy travelled to fetch the body and removed it from its rough wooden coffin at the *Hôpital Militaire*, placing it in another of oak which he had brought with him. Nemo was buried at Zellick, to the soft strains of 'La Brabançonne'.

A fortnight later came the order from Berlin for the execution of eleven heroes of the *Cantine Suédoise*: Emile Delbruyère, Antoine Renaud, Edouard Verpraet, Eric de Menten de Hornes, Jean Ingels, Albert Mélot, Henri Rasquin, Ghislain Neybergh, Gaston Bidoul, Robert Roberts Jones, the lawyer known as 'Y', and Georges Maréchal, the father of Elsie. At the foot of the document were the callous words:

'Clemency refused'

The execution of these faithful friends of Nemo was not long delayed. As Edith Cavell had been a generation before, they were shot at dawn at the Tir National in Brussels. The day before, Eric de Menten de Hornes wrote to his family:

> Tomorrow I shall make the great journey ... and you can be proud of me. I regret nothing. I die for the ideal we have all shared. Keep smiling.

Jean Ingels described the clothes he was wearing, so that his body could be identified after the war.

At 6 a.m. on 20 October, the Austrian chaplain of the prison, Monseigneur Gramman, at St Gilles brought them each two big hunks of bread and cheese. The wind howled and it was raining hard as they were taken to the Tir National, the rifle range of Brussels.

Eric de Menten smoked a cigarette and smiled and chatted with the guards who were to shoot him, and Commandant Bidoul's face had not lost its rosy, benevolent look. With Monseigneur Gramman they said their last prayers on that tragic, rainswept ground and lined up, their eyes unbandaged. The spirit of the *Cantine Suédoise* had remained to the end.

## Chapter Sixteen

## Franco

The inhabitants of the villa at Anglet continued in grave danger of arrest. Not that this worried Tante Go. She still bicycled everywhere with Janine. When arrests were made, she promptly found new helpers. That she and her family remained at liberty was partly due to the faithful l'Oncle, her husband, who skilfully covered her tracks through his position as interpreter to the Germans. Freddy, her son, worked with him. Together they continued to steal or counterfeit official stamps. They supplied *cartes d'identités* and passes for every region in the south of France.

The chestnut tree in the garden of the villa spread its pleasant shade. Beneath it, Tante Go and Janine sat knitting as they talked of the great days of the Line. Of Dédée and Paul there was no further news. The story of her last meeting with Nemo had filtered down the Line from Brussels. 'B' Johnson and the Lapeyres had reached England in safety. The hopes of all lay in Franco. It was he who would lead the Comet Line back to its former glories.

Fruit trees blossomed beside the stark, grey villa and waved lightly in the breeze. There was a sound of footsteps in the lane from the village. Tante Go rose and walked towards the house. She was anxious to reach the hiding place of her precious papers and official stamps. There was a loud knock. She signed to Janine to answer the door, and she stood out of sight.

In the doorway were two officers of the *Feldgendarmerie*.

'Is Madame De Greef here?'

'Yes.'

And Tante Go came inquiringly to the door. She looked innocent, unafraid.

'You must come with us. The Gestapo want to interview you.'

The Germans turned to Janine and said roughly:

'When your father returns, tell him that he is required this evening by the Gestapo.'

From a peg in the hall of the villa, Tante Go took her light raincoat. As she put it on, she turned to Janine. The two Germans still stood at the door, out of hearing.

'*Les papiers!*' she whispered.

Janine did not move. She knew exactly what to do. When her mother was led away along the lane, she ran to the secret hiding place. Here were kept, beside bank identity cards and stamps, all the accounts of the Line, with lists of rescued airmen.

With the papers in her handbag, she bicycled to the *Mairie* to warn her father. He was not there.

She searched for Freddy. A white-faced secretary came forward:

'I am afraid, Mademoiselle, your brother has just been arrested!'

Janine left the *Mairie* and hurried to Franco, who was staying with friends of Tante Go in the village. Breathlessly she cried.

'They have arrested my mother and Freddy!'

Franco was calm and debonair as usual.

'And your father?'

'The Gestapo told me to tell him when he returned that he was wanted at their office. Fortunately he is not at his job today.'

'Well, you must warn him when he comes back.'

Janine met her father on his return that evening. When he had heard his daughter's news, Monsieur De Greef had no intention whatever of going to the Gestapo. He repaired immediately to see his friend, a senior German officer of the *Kommandantur.* He stood in the office very tall and dark and spoke indignantly:

'Why are my wife and son arrested? I am only a poor refugee who earns his living as an interpreter. Sometimes, of course, we do a little black market, but nothing more!'

L'Oncle shrugged his shoulders. The German officer was red-faced and bald. He had stupid eyes. He was filled with sympathy for this valuable interpreter and his family.

He patted the agreeable but disconsolate l'Oncle on the shoulder.

'My poor friend, have no fear. They shall be released immediately.'

He took up the telephone, and the lanky Belgian smiled amiably. Then the German took a bottle of cognac from his office cupboard and set two glasses on the desk...

At midnight, Tante Go and Freddy were released. It was some time before they were able to discover the cause of their arrest. It seemed that copper-haired Tante Go and Janine, bicycling continually through the countryside, had excited suspicion.

'That was a near thing,' said Tante Go when she was back at the villa. 'There is nothing for it. I must go into *purdah* for a few weeks. I shall direct operations from here, but others will have to do the bicycling for the present.'

And a new recruit, Denise Houget, replaced her for a time.

Throughout the summer, Franco travelled back and forth every fortnight from Paris to Bilbao. Over France and Belgium the roar of heavy aircraft grew louder. In the twilight of great railways stations, the searchlight beams shone through glass roofs. Often the whine of a bomb could be heard as the steam hissed and the hushed crowds scrambled for shelter.

To Franco, the raids were stimulating. Each time an aircraft crashed, each time a parachute was seen to open, his enthusiasm for saving airmen increased. The Gare d'Austerlitz, where Dédée had so often led her charges, had become too dangerous. There were *gendarmes* and plain-clothes Gestapo at every barrier. The enemy was determined to control the routes to the coast.

It was necessary to escort the 'children' to Bordeaux and from there take a local train to Dax, not far from Bayonne. At Dax, bicycles were ready in the luggage office, and the men, sometimes escorted by Janine, sometimes by Franco, sometimes by Tante Go herself, would bicycle from Dax to Anglet.

The line to Bordeaux involved fourteen hours of travel by night in a crowded train. When they arrived, the men were met by Tante Go or one of her group and taken to a restaurant in the town. It had always been the policy of Dédée to feed the men well. It kept them quiet and contented. It prevented unforeseen incidents.

Tante Go, following this policy, would often take the men to a smart restaurant frequented by Germans. Restaurants with such a clientele could more easily acquire on the black market the rarest foods and wines. But in spite of this generosity, there was always the chance of a man endangering his rescuers and himself.

At one establishment where the *patron* was a loyal and devoted helper, it was the custom to order an excellent steak. Sitting one afternoon before taking the train to Dax, Tante

Go and three Allied airmen surveyed four splendid steaks, juicy and underdone. One of the airmen found the red flesh not to his liking.

'It is not cooked enough,' he complained.

Before she could stop him, the young man placed his plate on the floor and beckoned to a dog, which bounded eagerly towards it and began to eat.

Tante Go was horror-struck. In the summer of 1943, most human beings in Occupied France had almost forgotten the appearance of a beefsteak. She looked around the restaurant and observed the shocked countenances of the customers, and then, at the far end, she saw a German officer watching the scene in wide-eyed surprise.

Tante Go was tense. She watched the officer closely. He was taking a great interest. She toyed with her food, wondering what to do. Then the German rose to his feet and approached her table, smiling amiably, obviously bent on conversation. He spoke appalling French.

'I never thought the French were fond of animals. Let me congratulate you, *Monsieur.* Now in Germany... '

The airman shrank speechless into his corner, but Tante Go rose with a determined look.

'*Herr Oberleutnant*, I am afraid we have to go, or we will miss our train.'

She made signs to the airmen, who, disconsolately, left their meal.

The German was bewildered.

'But, madame, I only wished to convey my compliments on the excellent conduct of your friends towards this dog.'

He was an angular, lean individual and smiled awkwardly,

but Tante Go would not wait. She hustled the men into the street, where, at a decent distance from the restaurant, they upbraided their companion for the loss of their steaks.

Franco was at Dax, waiting on the platform to meet them. The bicycles were ready in the *consigne*. The travellers from Bordeaux, after the *débâcle* of the steak, were now confronted with a new difficulty. One of the airmen, an American, declared that he could not ride a bicycle.

'Well, we cannot leave you here,' said Franco. 'The bicycles must be returned to Anglet. You will have to learn.'

The American, after several painful falls on the *pavé*, began to follow the others unsteadily out of Dax. The town was crowded with workers and Germans, all on bicycles. The French workers in their blue smocks contrasted with the field-grey uniforms of the soldiers. In spite of much wobbling, the American reached the outskirts of Dax in safety.

They had twenty-six kilometres to travel to Bayonne and a long, white, featureless road stretched before them. The sun blazed down and, in its glare, they could see two dark objects steadily approaching in the opposite direction. Soon the figures of two cyclists appeared. They were German officers sitting very stiff and straight on their machines. The American seemed unnerved by their advance. He began to wobble violently and was unable to keep away from the left-hand side of the road.

'For Heaven's sake keep to the right!' shouted Franco. The American continued to zigzag painfully towards the Germans. A collision was inevitable. Tante Go and Franco prayed. The American had lost control. His bicycle was drawn to the Germans as if by a magnet. Their attempts to avoid him were of no avail, and he cannoned into them in the middle of the road. There was a clatter and a torrent of guttural swearing. The three of them lay in a heap. The smart uniforms and black polished boots of the officers were covered in white dust.

Franco was off his bicycle in an instant. He helped the officers to their feet and began to apologise profusely for the conduct of his comrade. He took from his pocket an empty cognac bottle.

'Look what this fellow has drunk! All in one gulp!'

He shook his head disapprovingly. The Germans spluttered. Their crimson faces expressed the deepest annoyance as they brushed the dust from their clothes. Franco shouted furiously at the discomfited American:

'You drunken fool. Look what you have done. You deserve to be shot!'

After a minute, honour was satisfied. The party went on their way, laughing, in spite of the embarrassment of this incident. Such was always the spirit of the Line. So it had always been in the days of Dédée.

By the autumn of 1943, Franco was exhausted. In addition to escorting the airmen in the train and on bicycles, he had constantly taken the arduous road to Bilbao since Dédée's arrest. Each time he returned to face new perils. At the end of September, the Consul at Bilbao persuaded him to stop. It was agreed that he should go to Gibraltar for a conference with officers of the British Intelligence Service.

As the big, black car with CD plates took him to Madrid, Franco had to confess to a sense of relief. For a week or more he would be away from occupied territory and under the protection of the British. He lay back with his head against the leather upholstery. It was tempting to feel that he could escape for a moment from the grim anxiety of his mission. And yet he never allowed himself to forget the vision of Dédée and the purpose of the Line. There came to him the memory of a winter's night when, on the Spanish side of the mountain, they had been together at a midnight Mass…

At Madrid he was transferred to another British car which hummed smoothly to Malaga and came to the frontier at La Linea. Franco was hidden in the luggage boot, crouching like the inmate of a burial urn. He was, luckily, slim and supple. He had been unceremoniously stowed inside two miles away from the frontier post.

The boot was closed with a bang and Franco was in overpowering heat and darkness. His last view had been the Rock standing supremely against a blue sky. The emerald and brown of its lower slopes gave it the look of a great inlaid stone rising above the sparkle of the sea. He had seen a squadron of fighters take off into the white haze over the Atlantic. And in the distance, beneath the shadow of Gibraltar, lines of battleships, lay imperturbable.

The heat grew and choked him as the car jolted over the rough road. In ten minutes it stopped, and Franco could hear voices in Spanish, and the Englishman who had driven him expostulating. He tried to imagine Customs officials examining papers and asking questions. Despite the heat and the discomfort, he could scarcely suppress a smile. To be travelling in the luggage boot of a diplomatic car reminded him of some forgotten melodrama of the Secret Service.

The engine hummed again, and in a quarter of an hour the car came to a halt. The boot was opened and Franco, choking and perspiring, scrambled into the cool air. He was in a courtyard in old Gibraltar. Through an archway he could see the flashing waters of the bay. Above him waved the Union Jack.

It was a great moment for Franco. There was the sound of boots on a wrought-iron staircase overgrown with leaves. A British officer wearing service dress came down to meet him. To Franco he seemed pink-faced and ordinary enough, disappointingly British. He bore no resemblance to Ashenden or Sir Percy Blakeney.

Franco found himself patted on the back, and his hand was shaken several times as he began to climb the staircase. He felt suddenly weary and sick, and the boils which had broken out on his neck began to pain him. The young officer spoke to him, with hearty assurance, in French, ignoring any refinements of accent or grammar.

'We have arranged for you to see the chief tomorrow.'

'I do not understand.'

'I mean the Governor.'

'The Governor of Gibraltar!'

Franco was half pleased, half dismayed. He imagined a superb reception beneath chandeliers with uniforms and decorations. After a pleasant dinner, he forgot his anxiety. His pain and weariness were gone.

Franco slept that night in great happiness. He awoke next morning to look out over the Atlantic and hear a few rounds fired by anti-aircraft guns. The Rock stood above him, impregnable and comforting. It gave him courage, but always before him was a vision. A long row of cells, and, at the end, with a clink of keys, a door opened and Dédée emerged in her prison dress. Then came a jailer taking her down innumerable stone steps to a Gestapo car...

And Franco, looking from the balcony to the flower-strewn garden below, said to himself:

'The Line must stay independent. We must remain faithful to her memory.'

The Governor of Gibraltar, Lieutenant-General Sir Noel Mason-MacFarlane, astonished Franco. He was a tall, white-haired man with a long, intelligent face. He was dressed in a bush shirt and khaki shorts. To the young Belgian, it was remarkable to be received by a representative of the King of England in shorts, but it put him at his ease. The Governor sat down at a table. He leaned on his elbows and looked hard at Franco. He spoke softly in excellent French.

'I am asked to thank you for all your brave work and to convey to all members of the Line the gratitude of the Allies. Tell them that the day of liberation will soon come.'

There was a silence, and Franco felt it hard to speak, so much had he been moved by the Governor's words. He sat there, looking very young and ascetic.

'We who work for the Line are only doing our duty by Belgium and France and the Allies,' he said.

Then the Governor rose and shook hands. Franco watched him pick up a General's cap with its scarlet band and walk away down the corridors of the Palace.

Franco had discovered in the British a new capacity for feeling. The interview with the Governor made them seem to him neither proud nor insular. As he surveyed the great fortress and its orderly calm, he felt for the first time that against these formidable people all the forces of Hitler would never prevail.

He was given a new suit and an identity card in the name of a British officer. He was allowed to see the fortress and the airfield. That evening the young officer spoke gently: 'Franco, you are ill. Why not come back to England for a few days? There you can rest, and go back when you are better.'

Franco looked at him.

'No, I will not leave. There are scores of pilots to bring through, and I am responsible.'

'We are sending you someone to help in Paris. Someone to replace Paul.'

'Who is he?' asked Franco doubtfully.

'We call him Jérôme.'

Franco was anxious. The Line had always been independent. The British had supplied money, but they had never controlled the Line.

He said urgently:

'But the Line remains independent? A French and Belgian Line?'

'Yes, of course. We will respect that.'

Two days later, refreshed and with a new-found strength, Franco climbed into the boot of the diplomatic car and crossed the frontier into Spain.

Within a week he was in Paris preparing to receive Jérôme, the new man from England.

# Chapter Seventeen

# Jacques Cartier

Count Antoine d'Ursel, alias Jacques Cartier, succeeded Nemo in Brussels, but from June 1943 he faced increasing peril. On the day when he betrayed Paul in Paris, Jean Masson made his way to Belgium with the Gestapo. On the night of 8 June, he brought about his second series of arrests. One after another the team, which Jacques Cartier had created after the arrest of Nemo, fell to the traitor. Jacques Cartier himself, escaping by a miracle, went into hiding during the summer.

The bombers came increasingly. The survivors doubled in number. The Line must be mended. It must never fail. Just as it had always been in the days of Dédée, so it must remain. And Jacques Cartier, from his hiding place, searched for new leaders. He found two staunch patriots, Jean Serment and his friend, Deltour. With Franco in the south, they formed yet another Line and, by vigorous effort, the flow of airmen from Brussels grew. In Paris, where it had seemed that all was lost, a new figure replaced Paul. He was a Belgian with straggling, blond hair and a rubicund face. He talked of farming and horses.

This was Count Jacques Legrelle, the 'Jérôme' of whom Franco was told at Gibraltar. He had, in 1940, escaped to England and there trained as a parachutist. One morning, he fell heavily on landing and broke his spine. He was many months in plaster but, undaunted, he undertook to help Franco. From

Gibraltar he travelled to Paris across the Pyrenees in the autumn of 1943.

Jérôme established his headquarters in Paris in a flat at the Rue de Longchamps. It was here that in the autumn Jacques Cartier came to discuss with Franco what he should do.

It was too dangerous for Jacques Cartier to return to Belgium. As the winter months wore on, he remained in Paris. It was his ambition to create a special line over the Pyrenees for Belgians who, like himself, had become known to the Gestapo and were obliged to flee to England.

The Comet Line, from that memorable August day in 1941 when Dédée first met the British at Bilbao, had been devoted to the rescue of trained pilots of the Allies. For those who were *brûlés*, hunted by the Gestapo for their underground work, there was no separate line. Cartier wished to raise this project with the British, and in December he resolved to escape to England.

On 23 December 1943, he arrived at Bayonne, and at Ciboure, among the gay cottages of fisher-folk, he hid in the house of Cataline Aguirre. With Franco he waited impatiently for Florentino. Then news came that the great guide was ill. Florentino ill! It seemed impossible to those who had worked so long with this extraordinary lord of the mountains that he could fail in strength. It was nothing serious, only an attack of influenza, but Florentino would not be able to guide them that night.

Late in the afternoon there was a scurrying to and fro among the hilly streets of Ciboure. At last, two smugglers, Manuel and Ramon, were found to guide the party, which included four American pilots. Then, warmed by the omelettes and harsh red wine of Cataline, eight men stepped softly across the Rue

Docteur Micé, which leads to the hills. With Franco and the two Basques at their head, they climbed up a frozen pathway.

It was a peaceful night. Franco hoped that even without Florentino they would cross in safety. Soon they reached the familiar points on the journey: the lighthouse of Fuenterrabia, the lights of Irun and the glimmer in the dark skies above San Sebastián. At two o'clock they began the steep descent to the tumbling Bidassoa. It had rained heavily the day before, and the river was high and in torrent. When they reached the bank, Franco and the guides conferred quickly. The roar of the water was around them. It was possible to cross, but the Americans and Cartier, who were not used to fording the river, would have to be helped, for it would be easy to fall and be carried away in the freezing rapids.

Manuel and Ramon and Franco then helped across the Americans, leaving Cartier on the French side. They made the crossing with difficulty. Often, one of the airmen and his guide were within a hair's breadth of being swept into the darkness. At length they were all across, with their trousers in bundles. They began to dress on the far bank.

Ramon returned to fetch Cartier, who was shivering violently. He was nearly fifty, and had spent much of his life in Indo-China. A bout of malaria shook his spare body. Yet he was determined to cross, and Ramon, taking him firmly by the arm, stepped with him into the river. Cartier felt the bitter cold of the water around him. His feet were on the rounded stones beneath. Suddenly he felt himself slipping. There was a loud splash and a cry and, with Ramon, he was carried along by the current.

The force of the water swept them apart, and Cartier, with

a great effort, clutched at the branch of a tree on the French side and painfully dragged himself to the bank. Ramon, the younger and stronger man, regained his balance and reached the anxious watchers on the Spanish side. It was a dangerous moment. The splashing and the cries might have alerted the Spanish frontier guards.

Franco, ordering the guides to take the Americans into Spanish territory, lay on the Spanish bank of the Bidassoa. He gave a low whistle, which was faintly answered from the other side. Then he struggled across and found Cartier lying exhausted and ill among the bushes. He was afraid that the older man could not continue. He knew that from now on the journey would be difficult. The slightest noise would result in an alert along the whole of the frontier. Crouching beside Cartier, he endeavoured to persuade him to return.

'Jacques, go back to the farmhouse two miles back. You can cross next time. The Americans will have to go on, but I will show you the way. You cannot cross tonight. It is too great a risk.'

Cartier's voice was weak, but he did not flinch.

'I will not go back. I must cross tonight. It would be foolish not to do so, after we have come all this way. Besides, it might be dangerous for you.'

Franco was filled with admiration. He, too, was soaked and chilled by the water. But he was young. He had made the crossing many times in all weathers.

'All right, then. *En route!*'

Franco had tied the legs of his trousers together in a knot round his neck so that they should keep dry. He now bade Cartier hang on to them from behind to keep his balance. He climbed down into the river, and once more felt the water swirling violently around him. Cartier had hardly stepped in behind him when there was the crack of rifle shots echoing down the valley.

'What is that?' gasped Cartier.

'The Spaniards are firing on the airmen,' said Franco in a low voice.

The sound of the shots ringing through the night seemed to throw Cartier off his balance. Franco had hardly moved five paces across the torrent when he felt a desperate tugging at his neck. There was a sigh as his companion slipped and, with a great splash, fell into the water. Franco, too, began to lose his footing. Then came a singing in his ears, and the next moment he was struggling desperately with the fierce current. He could hardly get his breath, and there was a sharp pain in his chest as he regained mastery. Suddenly he was swimming in calmer water, and struck out for the French bank. He had reached it before he realised that he was alone.

He lay there panting and horror-struck. He knew that Cartier was dead.

'Jacques!' he called desperately.

There was not a sound save the deep roar of the waters. Before him he could see the glimmer of the foam.

'Jacques!' he called again.

This time there came three angry stabbing rifle shots close at hand. Franco could see the orange flashes. He crawled miserably away from the French bank and, after an interval, started back from St Jean de Luz. At dawn he was at Ciboure with the terrible news. And Florentino, rising from his sickbed, exclaimed:

'If only I had been there!'

Later in the day came news of further disasters. The guides had escaped, but three of the Americans had been taken prisoner when they were fired on. The fourth, John Burch, in his flight, had fallen into the Bidassoa and was drowned. His body was found the next day with that of Cartier near Irun. They were both buried in secret by the Germans. Already the Basque population had learned of the disaster and had begun to bring flowers to the spot where they lay.

So perished the gallant Count Antoine d'Ursel, alias Jacques Cartier, the successor of Nemo. At the spot where he was drowned in the Bidassoa a white cross stands today on the French bank amid the scrubby bushes where Franco had called despairingly against the wind:

'Jacques! Jacques!'

The month of December had been one of brilliant success, and already 300 pilots and soldiers of the Allies had crossed the mountains, but Christmas 1943 was clouded by this bitter tragedy. Franco would never forget that terrible night. He was already tired and ill from his exertions. He felt the net closing around him. For him the end would not be long. Only by prayer was he sustained.

Early in January, the Gestapo, for the third time, searched the flat of Jean Serment, the new chief in Brussels. Other helpers of the new organisation received visits from those square-jawed inquisitors. One of those who fled to safety was a remarkable childlike figure. Her name was Lily Dumont, sister of the Nadine who had worked for Paul. She was known in the organisation as 'Michou'.

Michou was tiny, pink-cheeked and innocent, but a brave and reliable guide. On 7 January 1943, she left her home in

Brussels for the last time, and reached Paris. There she told Jérôme of her danger. In a few days she reached Bayonne.

The sands were fast running out. There were anxious conferences in Brussels and Paris. Jérôme, Franco, Deltour and Jean Serment shook hands and wondered, as Nemo and Dédée had done, if they would ever meet again.

Jérôme had already decided that he could not continue. To stay meant disaster and, after a visit to Brussels, he returned to the flat at the Rue de Longchamps to prepare for his return to England. He was too late. Jean Masson was back.

On the evening of 17 January 1944, Jérôme opened the door of the flat with his key. There was a violent movement around him, and four men leapt from the chairs where they had been sitting with drawn revolvers, shouting:

'German Secret Police. Put up your hands.'

Jérôme stood in the middle of the room with his untidy blond hair and his care-worn expression. He had bravely faced the gnawing fear which he had felt all the six months of his life in Paris. And now it had come. He determined at every cost not to betray Franco. He was taken to the Gestapo office in Rue des Saussaies, where Paul and the others had suffered before him. They interrogated him for five hours at a stretch on the night of his arrest, putting to him always the same vital question:

'Where is Franco?' They beat him, but he refused to reply, for Franco had seemed to Jérôme a man of infinite faith and leadership. He knew that if Franco were to be caught there would be nothing left. Jérôme hoped to gain time. He longed to survive until the Allies landed in France. He therefore faced the bullying and the torture so that the Comet Line might end in victory. They shouted at him again:

'Where is Franco? Come on, talk, you bastard!'

And yet Jérôme, who had often been afraid, did not flinch. He was convinced that Franco would get away, that he would be warned before he returned to the flat at the Rue de Longchamps…

As he sat in the train on the way back to Paris from Brussels, where he had conferred with Jean Serment on that same night of 17 January, Franco was wondering how long it would be before the next blow fell. He had been, apart from Tante Go, the moving spirit of the Line from Paris to Bilbao since the arrest of Dédée a year before. In that time the Line had been broken and mended many times. More than fifty people had been arrested. With the death of Jacques Cartier, the death roll of Comet had risen to twelve.

Would he be the next? Franco, young and dignified, was not afraid. He thought of the ironic end of Nemo, killed by an Allied bomb. Then there was Eric de Menten de Hornes and those he had known in the happy days in Brussels before he entered the Line. What had happened to Paul and Robert Aylé? There had been little news since the announcement that they were condemned to death by court martial. They were still in Paris, but Germaine Aylé had been sent to Germany. And Dédée? Where was the Little Cyclone now? Was she alive or dead? Some said she was in Germany. The bright memory of her sustained his courage.

At eight o'clock in the morning of 18 January, Franco left the train at the Gare du Nord and went straight to the Rue de Longchamps.

As he walked to the door, he had a sharp presentiment that danger lay within. It seemed to draw him to the door. He had hardly rang the bell before they were on him. He tried to parry their questions, but they knew him.

'How are you, Franco? We are pleased to meet you at last.'

They took him, as they had done the rest, to the Rue des Saussaies, where he sat facing the same hard-faced Germans who had beaten Jérôme the night before. When he was waiting outside the interrogation room, a young man with fair hair and cold blue eyes, with suppressed fury in them, entered the room. Franco knew at once that it was Jean Masson, though they had never met. Jean Masson walked over to him and looked down at him with a hatred in his eyes that astonished Franco.

'I am Jean Masson,' said the young man, 'and it is I who have betrayed all of you.'

He spoke with a kind of insane pride, and his laughter was horrible. Franco was sad. He was a man of deep religious faith, who believed in charity and frankness. When Franco had been released, desperately ill, from a concentration camp, he came face to face with Jean Masson again. The tables were turned. Jean Masson would soon be executed in Paris as a traitor. But Franco forgave him, for he was a man of God. Franco knew that Jean Masson had been illegitimate and had never known a proper home, that he had grown up with bitterness in his soul. Such was the way of the traitor.

One more surprise awaited Franco. A slim, elegant Gestapo official came up to him. He had a long, sharp nose, and his lips were pale and twisted.

'Well, Franco, why did you take the seals off the door at the Rue Vaneau?'

'I have not been to the Rue Vaneau for months.'

'Don't lie! You had better think this over.'

But Franco had ceased to think of the questions he would be asked about the Rue Vaneau. He stared at the German. And then his face broke into a strange, baffling smile.

'What are you grinning at, Franco? Things look bad for you.'

'Oh, nothing.'

Franco thought that if ever he were free again, it would be delightful to explain why he was laughing. The man from the Gestapo was wearing his long-lost favourite tie, which he had searched for at the Rue Vaneau after Paul's arrest in June of the previous year.

## Chapter Eighteen

# Tail of the Comet

In one week nearly all the members of Comet in Brussels and Paris were arrested. In the south, Tante Go hungered for news. At Anglet, with Monsieur De Greef and Janine, she prepared for the worst. After all these years, would she and her family outlive the latest storm? There was nothing to do but wait.

The flame of treason was about to leap to her very door. In Paris and Brussels, Jean Masson was waiting to strike. He had mingled once again with the remnants of the Line under the name of Pierre Boulin. When Lily Dumont, alias Michou, sister of the Andrée Dumont who had worked for Paul, reached Paris in February, he presented himself and proposed that a new line should be formed. He was facile and optimistic. He spoke to her encouragingly, offering all manner of assistance, as he had done to Paul. Michou was delighted with his boldness. She told him she would go to Spain to regain contact with the British. They arranged to meet at the beginning of March, when she returned.

Little Michou, only just five feet in height, was sturdy and determined. She spoke in a soft, childish voice. Her face was round and artless like her sister Nadine's. She looked no more than fifteen, an advantage which she used to the full. She was a worshipper of Dédée, willing to undergo every danger. She was thrilled with her mission. She crossed into Spain on 28 February 1944. As they had been three years before when Little Cyclone had first appeared, the British were sceptical of her plans to continue the Line. But they sent her back to France, where she learned from Tante Go of fresh arrests in Paris.

Among them was Martine, a woman dentist. This brave Frenchwoman was Michou's friend and companion. She had been free from contact with the ill-fated group of Franco. What had gone wrong? In Michou's mind, suspicion of treachery grew as she talked to Tante Go. Both Martine and she had met the persuasive, blue-eyed 'Pierre Boulin'.

'I am going back to Paris,' said Michou suddenly.

'But where? There is nothing left there or in Brussels,' said Tante Go.

After four crowded years there was no one left of that famous band who had worked with Tante Go. She had seen disaster follow disaster, and always the Line had risen anew. Yet, tough as she was, there were tears for her to shed. What of Dédée, Franco and Jean Dassié, with his simple courage?

Michou was adamant. Even the commanding Tante could not restrain her.

'There is a traitor in the Line, and I am going to find out who it is.'

And Michou, taking the train to Paris, went straight to Fresnes prison. Sitting in a tram, she was like a schoolgirl returning home from class. Her feet barely touched the floor of the tram. Who would have supposed that this was the foremost courier of the Line? Who would have thought her on a mission of life or death?

The method she adopted to find the name of the traitor was

characteristic. She left the tram and walked to the very walls of the prison. She found a point where she could observe the women's quarter. She stood there and studied the scowling lines of narrow windows. Which was Martine's cell? She had no idea. Then in her loudest voice she cried out:

'Martine! Martine!'

A shrill voice answered from within. It was Martine. Michou cried again with all her might:

'Martine! Who is the traitor? Who has betrayed you?'

The voice from the prison called again. It was unearthly, echoing across the cheerless prison courtyard. A voice from the other side.

'It is Pierre! It is Pierre!'

As she stood beneath the prison wall, Michou understood.

It is Pierre Boulin! He and Jean Masson are the same. I must hurry to warn Tante Go! And to think that next week I have my rendezvous with him: that suave, blond traitor with blue eyes!

On that March afternoon, Michou ran down the street. There were shouts behind her. A *gendarme* beckoned. There was nothing for it but to stop.

'*Mademoiselle*, you must come with me. I shall take you before the Commandant for communicating with a prisoner.'

Michou looked naughty and said nothing. She was taken before the Commandant. He studied her round face and her hair tied with pink ribbon. He was mystified.

'How old are you?'

'I am fifteen.'

'Yes, that is what your identity card says. What are you doing on your own in Paris? You come from the south, *Mademoiselle?*'

The Commandant was kindly and polite. His daughter was fifteen.

'Yes, I live in the south, but I was told to visit the dentist who has looked after me for a long time. When I got to her house, I heard that she had been arrested. I wanted to ask her if I could do anything for her.'

'But what,' spluttered the Commandant, 'did you think you could do for her?'

'My mother,' replied Michou simply, 'would, no doubt, have liked to send her a parcel.'

The Commandant could not repress a smile. He waved a finger reprovingly at Michou.

'*Mademoiselle*, I am letting you off this time, but do not do this kind of thing. You are released on account of your youth, but make sure you do not come here again, and be sure to return immediately to your mother.'

He twirled his little moustache and then took up his papers and laughed amiably.

'Only fifteen! Very naughty!'

And Michou, smiling shyly, walked out of the prison and took the train to Bayonne to report her vital news. It was her action which saved Tante Go and the whole of the organisation in the south. They were to survive until the great day when the Allies landed in Normandy.

As for the extraordinary Michou, she still defied the enemy. She continued as a guide. For several weeks after her visit to the prison she escorted men from Paris, and twice more crossed the Pyrenees. She was a worthy successor to Elsie and Peggy, to Elvire Morelle and Madeleine Bouteloupt, bold disciples of

Dédée who now suffered in her cause. No one knew whether they were alive or dead.

Dédée had become a legend, a symbol of service and defiance. To these young women she had been the source of their determination to brave perils that few women had done before. She had given them their sense of devotion to the Line, and with it equality with men who undertook the same tasks. It was always Dédée's Line, even to the cool, authoritative Tante Go.

But Michou had to flee. She had ignored every hazard. The delightful impudence of her exploits made her suspect. After much debate and many tears, she was induced to cross the Pyrenees for the third and last time along the well-worn route of Dédée and Florentino. Even in prosaic England, now organising for the great assault, her fire was unquenched. She could not forget the splendid adventure of the Line. She feared for Nadine, her sister, and her parents, Monsieur and Madame Dumont, all prisoners of Hitler. She volunteered to train as a parachutist, but the British politely but firmly refused. The next few months were a time of cruel inactivity for her.

For Tante Go, too, these were sad days. The Line recovered fitfully after Franco's arrest. She fretted in the villa at Anglet. There seemed little left but memories. She was the *doyenne* of the Line. Only she was left of those historic personalities from France and Belgium who had so much helped the Allied cause. She had delighted in her work of commanding the troops of the south. She was still young-looking, forceful and clever. But, as she mused in the villa on winter nights, her world seemed to have changed. She was filled with frustration and annoyance. Her green eyes expressed impatience. What was everyone waiting for? Everywhere Occupied Europe waited tensely for signs from over the Channel.

On 28 March 1944 came poignant news for the watchers at Anglet. Frédéric De Jongh, alias Paul, the frail and gentle schoolmaster, was led from his cell at Fresnes to Mont-Valérien. He understood his own impractical, scholarly nature. He had been ill-equipped to follow the dynamic Dédée. But he loved her. He had no regrets. He was proud to have stayed the course. Before he died he was received into the Church.

In his last hours he asked to be with Robert Aylé and Aimable Fouquerel, the *masseur* of the Rue Oudinot. They sat at the same table and wrote their final letters. And then, on a fine morning at dawn, before Paris had gone to work or children were ready for school, the Belgian and the two Frenchmen died together, smiling.

Paul had been his daughter's most faithful servant. He was a martyr of the Line. And every year, on 28 March, the children of the École Frédéric De Jongh in Brussels place flowers on his memorial and sing 'La Brabançonne'.

Tante Go had little time for grief at her countryman's death. Already the fleets of the Allied Air Force swept across the skies to France in preparation for the great landing. Though it was the dawn of their liberation, Tante Go and her family worked on. The Line resumed and parties of airmen, led by Florentino, went to Spain, but the savage bombing of road and rail communications made it unsafe to bring more than a few from Paris. It was not worth the risk. Orders came from London to concentrate the men in groups in Belgium and Central France.

By the Sherwood Plan of the Marathon Mission, the airmen were gathered from their hiding places by the few remaining helpers and grouped in forests. Over 100 hid in the forest of Freteval near Châteaudun, and as many camped out in the thick woods of the Ardennes. There they stayed, in their 'camps', until their liberation in August and September 1944. They were supplied with food and clothing by parachute or by audacious black marketeering. Their morale was sustained by the stirring news of the Allied advance brought by agents dropped to them. As a result of this skilful operation, hardly a man was lost when the Allies finally broke through and rescued them. It was a fit ending to the great Comet Line.

Tante Go heard the furious bombing by day and night as she continued to keep contact with her organisation. The escape line was virtually at an end, but a few parties still went over the Pyrenees at the very moment of invasion. Then came the great battle of Normandy.

Tante Go was irrepressible. She had already sent Janine across the mountains for safety, but she and Monsieur De Greef continued their underground exploits to the very last. When there were no airmen, they took to espionage. Three times she crossed the familiar frontier, in person, carrying secret details of German dispositions. The British begged her not to return. She had been very gallant, they said. Why risk all when the war was nearly over? But Tante Go would have none of it. She would see the beginning and the end of this immortal story. And in those last days there was a fantastic incident in the best tradition of the Line.

Florentino had climbed unceasingly to and fro for three years from St Jean de Luz to the lowlands on the Spanish side. He had helped to bring through over 200 airmen to safety. After the landing in Normandy, he still marched nimbly over the frontier, crossing the Bidassoa, and skirting the Trois Couronnes until he could see the Spanish coast. It was a month after D-Day that he made his last passage, taking with him, instead of airmen, minute pieces of paper, messages for Allied Intelligence. After delivering them, he set off as usual on return to France.

At three o'clock in the morning, Florentino had crossed the Bidassoa and was descending to Urrugne. Suddenly in the night there was the rapid fire of an automatic weapon. He fell, with one leg shattered and bleeding. He felt a furious pain, but, alert as ever, he took from his tunic the secret papers which he was carrying and slipped them beneath a boulder. Then, despite the agony of his leg, he began to roll over and over in the darkness down a slope. The shouts of Germans came nearer. In the end they found him. They stood over him asking questions.

He did not reply. He bore his pain in silence as, with difficulty, they carried him to a frontier post. From there he was taken by car to the Police Headquarters at Hendaye. He was lifted clumsily from the car and laid on the floor of the office.

'Name?'

Florentino lay with his eyes closed. There was no answer. They asked him in French and Spanish and in the Basque language through interpreters. Not a word would he speak. After scratching their heads, the Germans dispatched him to the civilian hospital at Bayonne. One of his legs was hideously fractured, the bone broken in 100 pieces.

The news reached Tante Go. She was mad for action, and responded with her old fire. Within twenty-four hours she had, through numerous contacts and friends, acquired full details of the incident. She knew where Florentino was lying in the hospital. She knew the ward and the number of his bed.

Beside Florentino lay a young Frenchman injured in a recent bombardment. When Tante Go had discovered his name, she planned to visit him, bringing him a parcel of cakes and fruit. One morning she boldly entered the ward, walked to the young man's bed, and stood beside him.

Florentino did not move. He gave no sign of recognition. For half an hour Tante Go sat beside him talking to the young man, who was delighted with his visitor. Then, as she rose to go, she dropped her handbag; As she bent down between the beds to pick it up, she whispered in Spanish:

'Two o'clock.'

Still Florentino did not move. He lay there like a man in a dream. He had spoken little, even to the nuns who tended his wound. He was determined to give no information to anyone.

At two o'clock there was noise and commotion at the far end of his ward. Loud voices in German frightened the patients. Three stern-looking men stood arguing with the Sisters of Mercy.

'He cannot be moved. It would be dangerous!' cried the nuns.

The men brushed aside these protests. One of them waved a paper. The others rudely pushed past the nuns. Their hats still remained firmly on their heads, as was the custom of the Gestapo. They marched up to Florentino's bed and informed him in German, of which he understood not a word, that he was to be transferred to another hospital.

Florentino remained impassive, his big, gnarled hands resting on the sheets. His lined, weatherbeaten face was without expression. A stretcher was brought, and with much ado he was hastily lifted on to it. The men carried him from the ward. The voices of the Sisters of Mercy had risen in anger:

'You brutes!' screamed one of them, sobbing.

As they carried Florentino from the entrance to a waiting ambulance, the whole staff of the hospital gathered at the door. There were cries of:

'Barbarians!'

'So that is how you treat wounded! You wait till the Allies get here!'

'Have you no mercy on this poor man?'

The Gestapo was in a hurry, and handled the stretcher roughly, to shouts of:

'*Los! Los! Schnell!*'

Their behaviour, even for the Gestapo, was brutal and outrageous. The faces of all three bore an unpleasant sneer. Their hair was cropped. Their eyes stared fiercely.

Their sinister appearance seemed not to affect Florentino. He was bundled into the ambulance like a sack of flour. He must have suffered agony, but he said not a word. After a last display of bad manners and guttural shouting, the ambulance drew out of the courtyard of the hospital and disappeared. The tearful group of nuns wrung their hands as they stood on the steps. The taciturn, brown-skinned Florentino had been their favourite.

Despite the jolting of the ambulance as it sped along the road to Anglet, Florentino was grinning broadly. The 'Gestapo' had now removed their hats, and shook each other by the hand. They offered Florentino a welcome glass of cognac, which he drained immediately. They no longer spoke German, and the scowl had disappeared from their faces. Florentino had easily recognised their leader. It was the gallant l'Oncle, the husband of Tante Go, and two of his friends.

As a result of his position as interpreter in the *Mairie* at Anglet, Monsieur De Greef had concocted and forged an order from the Gestapo for the transfer of Florentino from Bayonne to Biarritz. Armed with these documents, he had requisitioned one of the municipal ambulances of Bayonne.

The rescue of Florentino took only twenty minutes. Within the same period of time he was safely hidden in a house on the outskirts of the village of Anglet. It was here that in a few weeks he was liberated by the Allies he had served so well. But lack of skilled surgery had left his leg deformed. His liberators sent him to hospital in Paris. It was, alas, impossible to prevent one leg being longer than the other.

Florentino was a monarch of the mountains. He belonged to the wild atmosphere of the heights. He lived his life among the blue and green and gold of the hills. No longer would he walk with his masterful air over the rocky paths and whisper hoarsely:

'*Espere un poco.*'

Yet he can still laugh, as he drinks a glass of wine, over those nights when the going was hard. For him the lashing of the rain was a spur to the conquest of the hills. To the struggling and exhausted British and American airmen who cried out for rest he would say:

'*Dos cent metros!*'

Those eternal '*dos cent metros*' when the way was slippery and dark! Florentino lives at Ciboure with his memories of Tante Go and 'B' Johnson and Franco and many others.[†] Yet there was one who surpassed all in her greatness. He will talk to you of Dédée in his strange mixed language until the dawn rises over the fishing vessels in the bay of St Jean de Luz. He

---

†    Florentino died in July 1980 and is buried at Ciboure.

speaks of her with awe, walking more strongly than any man, encouraging them, driving them on through the night...

As for clever, neat Tante Go, she was soon to lay down her command. The end came when, in July 1944, a Dakota landed on the aerodrome at Biarritz: Tante Go and her husband were there to meet it. Out of it stepped their children and faithful 'B' Johnson. Then there was a reunion of all her group in the villa at Anglet, that ugly little house that had seen so much of tragedy and triumph.

# Epilogue

For months after the liberation of France and Belgium, Little Cyclone and other members of Comet suffered in the foul concentration camps of Germany. In May 1945, many had already died. It was a long time before the full toll was known. Of the hundreds of helpers who had been imprisoned, twenty-three were shot. One hundred and thirty-three perished of starvation and brutality, victims of Hitler's New Order. They had helped to save more than 800 men of the Allies. Such was the price.

From filthy Ravensbrück and Mauthausen and Dachau emerged a proud but pitiful band. The first group of women were transported direct to Switzerland. They were no more than skeletons. Dressed in their macabre prison clothes, they seemed to have been literally rescued from the grave. At their head was staunch Elvire Morelle, pale and emaciated but still composed. There was Andrée Dumont, alias Nadine, the sister of Michou. Her father had already disappeared forever in the grisly toils of Himmler's programme of mass extermination.[†]

Next in this pathetic cortège came widowed Madame

---

[†]    Among the survivors from Mauthausen, two who must also be mentioned are Miss Elisabeth Liégeois and Mrs Elisabeth Warnon, who lodged thirty-five Allied airmen at the time of the *Cantine Suédoise*. They were condemned to death in 1943.

Maréchal and Elsie, dreadfully thin, and white as corpses. The horror of that moment when the false Americans had cried 'The game is up!' still stood in their eyes.

There were others, like Martine, the courageous woman dentist of Paris, to whom the incredible Michou, outside Fresnes Prison, had cried shrilly:

'Martine! Martine! Who is the traitor?'

Gentle, brown-eyed Madeleine Bouteloupt, her strength exhausted, was carried to her home in Paris and died on VE day itself.

Then came the men. Arnold Deppé of the famous crossing of the Somme, and Jacques Legrelle, alias Jérôme, returned like ghosts from the past. They have both lived through those anguished days, and went on to lead useful and happy lives.

On 18 May 1945, Charlie Morelle, the sparkling Frenchman, lay dying on his hospital bed at Dachau. Around him were the gruesome sheeted shapes of his companions. There was a dreadful, overpowering smell of disinfectant. A faint stir in the silent ward, and the sharp tap of military boots on the floor. Charlie raised himself weakly. A smart figure in French uniform walked up to his bed. Dimly, Charlie saw the salute and smiled. It was General Leclerc.

*'Bonjour, mon Lieutenant.'*

*'Bonjour, mon Général.'*

Charlie watched the General for a moment. Then peacefully he fell asleep, and died within a few hours.

Where was Franco, the brilliant successor of Dédée on the voyages over the mountains? He, too, had suffered desperately. He was at the very gates of death. For months he lingered, the victim of tuberculosis, but nothing destroyed his faith. Today he continues in the service of God, for as soon as he had recovered he entered the priesthood.[†]

However great their pain, the survivors of the Comet Line thought always of Dédée. She had, like them, undergone the horrors of the camp where, with Suzanne Wittek, she was imprisoned for nearly two years. When she arrived in Switzerland, a special car driven by 'B' Johnson was sent to fetch her and her sister to Belgium. She lay in hospital, dangerously ill, but her courage was undimmed. It was with difficulty that she was restrained from leaving her bed to help others who were in need.

The Allies set up Awards Bureaux in Brussels and Paris. The British alone distributed 8,000 letters of thanks on parchment to the people of Belgium and France. Numerous OBEs, MBEs, BEMs and King's Medals were given to those who had sheltered and fed escapers.

Franco got a DSO for he was a lieutenant in the Belgium Army. The George Medal, the highest award which could be given by Great Britain to a civilian, was awarded to Michou, Tante Go and Dédée.

In 1946, Dédée came to London to receive her decoration. With her mother, she went to Buckingham Palace, and was received by both Their Majesties. For many days, she was fêted and decorated by the Americans, the French and her own countrymen. The Royal Air Force presented her with a clock designed from the cockpit of a bomber.

She never lost her modest charm. Today she is thirty-eight and training to be a nurse. She is studying tropical medicine so

---

†     Franco died on 6 June 2008, aged eighty-nine.

that, despite her loss of health, she can serve in the Congo. In her white uniform, she is small and reserved, until she speaks of the shining days of Comet. When she recalls how the enemy lay in wait for her on every side, she is transformed by some inner grace and power.

Like Franco and her father she has turned to God. She still shows her old contempt for pain and fear. Her full, blue eyes are watchful and alert. She tells with laughter of hair's-breadth escapes.

Dédée speaks of her selfless life without passion, for she is a woman of true greatness. Sometimes she sits silent, with her fine, sensitive hands clasped before her.

Is it of Paul that she is thinking, dressed in his raincoat and beret as he leaves the Rue Vaneau on his last tragic journey to meet the traitor? Or of brave Charlie Morelle, with his long, sharp, humorous nose? Is it of magnificent Nemo, who now rests among the orchards of Zellick? Does she dream of the black nights with Florentino when the rain lashed down among the rocks and only her own fiery spirit drove the men forward to freedom? Or is it of that hot day in August 1941, when she swept into the Consulate at Bilbao and the Comet Line began?[†]

---

[†]　Andrée De Jongh worked for many years as a nurse in Africa, serving in the Belgian Congo, Cameroon, Ethiopia and Senegal. She died on 13 October 2007.

# Members of the Comet Line
# Killed in Action

Charles ANDRIEU died in
Buchenwald concentration camp
on 17 August 1944, aged 40
Céline ARNOULD died in
Ravensbrück concentration
camp in April 1945, aged 62
Rosalie ARNOULD-LOIR died
in Mauthausen concentration
camp on 20 March 1945,
aged 32
Renée ASTIER de VILATTE disappeared in Germany in 1944–45,
aged 46
Elise AUBANEL died in
Ravensbrück concentration
camp on 24 April 1945,
aged 46
Robert AYLÉ was shot in Paris on
28 March 1944, aged 44
Germaine BAJPAI died in
Ravensbrück concentration camp
on 4 February 1945, aged 50
Ferdinand BEAU died in Auschwitz
concentration camp on 15 May
1944, aged 49
Marguerite BEAUVAIS died in
Ravensbrück concentration
camp in 1944–45, aged 59
Renée BEAUVAIS died in
Ravensbrück concentration
camp in 1944–45, aged 32

Marguerite BENOIT died in
Ravensbrück concentration
camp in January 1945, aged 65
Jacques BERTELS died at
Neuengamme concentration
camp on 27 December 1944,
aged 44
Charles BERTRAND was killed at
Beverloo on 6 September 1944,
aged 42
Gaston BIDOUL was shot in Brussels
on 20 October 1943, aged 61
Raymond BIERNAUX died in
Neuengamme concentration
camp on 3 March 1945, aged 20
Madeleine BOUTELOUPT died in
Paris from effects of captivity on
7 May 1945, aged 33
Marie-Thérèse BOUVY died at
Ravensbrück concentration
camp in January 1945, aged 36
Jean BOY died in Germany on
6 April 1945, aged 48
Guillaume BRAUN was shot in
Germany on 21 June 1943, aged 55
Lambertine BRONCKAERT died
in Bergen-Belsen concentration
camp in April 1945, aged 54
Elisabeth BUFFET died in
Ravensbrück concentration
camp in March 1945, aged 52

Bernard BULTEEL died in Ellrich concentration camp in February 1945, aged 35

Antoinette BURY died in Ravensbrück concentration camp on 17 December 1943, aged 56

Edith van CAMPENHOUT died in Ravensbrück concentration camp in February 1945, aged 67

Baronne Louise CHAUDOIR died in Ravensbrück concentration camp in March 1945, aged 67

Jean CHAUVEAU was shot by the Germans at Châteaudun at the end of 1944, aged 30

Pierre CLAES disappeared in Auschwitz concentration camp in 1944–45, aged 62

Jules COLLE was shot in Germany on 30 September 1944, aged 33

Lucien COLLIN was shot at Ludwigsburg on 30 June 1944, aged 35

José CRACCO died in Flossenbürg concentration camp in March 1945, aged 34

Marie-Louise van CRAEN died in Ravensbrück concentration camp in March 1945, aged 49

Marcel DAELEMANS died in Neuengamme concentration camp on 17 December 1944, aged 43

Jean DASSIÉ died in Paris from effects of captivity 29 May 1945, aged 50

Marie-Louise DAVREUX died in Ravensbrück concentration camp on 24 December 1944, aged 64

Marguerite DEBERTRAND died in Ravensbrück concentration camp in February 1945, aged 57

Henri DECAT was killed in the Soignes Forest on 13 February 1943, aged 32

Cécile DECKERS died in Ravensbrück concentration camp in February 1945, aged 47

Emile DELBRUYERE was shot in Brussels on 20 October 1943, aged 30

Jean-François DELEU disappeared in Germany in 1944–45, aged 20

Marceline DELOGE died in Ravensbrück concentration camp on 3 February 1944, aged 67

Pierre DENEUVILLE disappeared during the liberation of Belgium, aged 23

Edmond DERYCK died at Kassel on 7 February 1945, aged 42

Maurice DESSON died in Meppen concentration camp on 10 March 1945, aged 40

Marie DETAILLE died in Ravensbrück concentration camp in February 1945, aged 63

Victor DETAILLE was shot in Bochum concentration camp on 19 April 1944, aged 58

Joséphine DETHIER died in Ravensbrück concentration camp in 1944, aged 54

Henri DEVLEESCHOUWER died in Germany on 26 April 1945, aged 53

Marie-Madeleine DEWE died in Ravensbrück concentration camp on 17 January 1945, aged 30

Emile DIDIER died in Gross-Rosen concentration camp on 15 January 1945, aged 55

Madeleine DIDIER died in Ravensbrück concentration camp in February 1945, aged 52

Pierre van DINTER was shot in Ludwigsburg on 19 April 1944, aged 50

Baron Jacques DONNY was shot at Stuttgart on 29 February 1944, aged 59

Jules DRICOT was killed between Magdeburg and Dessau in April 1945, aged 31

Florence DUCHENE disappeared in Ravensbrück concentration camp after being arrested in September 1941, aged 35

Eugène DUMONT disappeared in Gross-Rosen concentration camp in early 1945, aged 50

Alexandre ELISSALDE died in France from effects of captivity on 23 November 1946, aged 52

Léon FOUARD died in Mauthausen concentration camp on 4 March 1945, aged 48

Raymonde FOUCHE died in Ravensbrück concentration camp in February 1945, aged 35

Aimable FOUQUEREL shot in Paris on 28 March 1944, aged 40

Jean de FROTTE disappeared in Germany in 1944–45, aged 25

Arthur GEORGES died at Silsburg on 19 May 1944, aged 34

Jean-Baptiste GORIS disappeared in Gross-Rosen concentration camp after being arrested in 1943, aged 48

Carlos GOUBAU died at Neuengamme concentration camp on 5 March 1945, aged 23

Abbé Jules GRANDJEAN died in Gross-Rosen concentration camp on 11 February 1945, aged 45

Baron Jean GREINDL was killed by Allied bombing in prison at Etterbeek, on 7 September 1943, aged 38

Abel GUIDET died in Gross-Rosen concentration camp on 27 January 1944, aged 54

Maurice GUIGON died in the Saint Gilles Prison, Brussels, on 25 June 1943, aged 54

Georges GUILLON died in Mauthausen concentration camp on 22 April 1945, aged 54

Charlotte HAFFERBOURGER died in Ravensbrück concentration camp in April 1945, aged 59

Eugène d'HALLENDRE was shot in Lille on 27 December 1943, aged 45

Jean-François van den HOVE died at Essen on 5 August 1943, aged 42

Eugène HUBEAU was shot in Brussels on 17 September 1943, aged 41

Jean INGELS was shot in Brussels on 20 October 1943, aged 36

Baronne Elisabeth de JAMBLINNE de MEUX died in Ravensbrück concentration camp in March 1945, aged 52

Marcel JONCKHEERE was shot in Berlin on 6 August 1945, aged 39

Frédéric de JONGH was shot in Paris on 28 March 1944, aged 56

Joséphine LACROIX died in Essen
in March 1945, aged 59

Berthe LAMBRECHT died in
Neuengamme concentration
camp in 1944, aged 57

Vassili LAMI disappeared in
Neuengamme concentration
camp in 1944, aged 30

René LAMMERS died in Bochum
concentration camp in April
1945, aged 46

Jean LARBURU disappeared in
Germany in March 1944,
aged 31

Jean LAROY died in Flossenbürg
concentration camp on 10 April
1945, aged 43

Léon LEYNEN disappeared in
Gross-Rosen concentration
camp in 1944–45, aged 35

Georges LUCAS disappeared
in Germany in March 1945,
aged 24

Henri MACHIELS died in Upper
Silesia on 10 December 1944,
aged 47

Clara MACHTOU disappeared in
Germany following his arrest
in 1943, aged 25

Augusta MARCOUX died in
Bergen-Belsen concentration
camp on 21 May 1945,
aged 37

Georges MARÉCHAL was shot in
Brussels on 20 October 1943,
aged 50

Louis MASSINON died in Gross-
Strelitz concentration camp after
his arrest in 1942, aged 42

Christine MAUROIT died in
Ravensbrück concentration
camp in February 1945, aged 39

Eugène MAYNE died at Sulingen
on 2 May 1945, aged 31

Maurice MEHUDIN died in
Flossenbürg concentration camp
after his arrest in 1943, aged 39

Albert MÉLOT was shot in Brussels
on 20 October 1943, aged 27

Auguste MELOT died in
Neuengamme concentration
camp on 6 November 1944,
aged 73

Marguerite MELOT died in
Ravensbrück concentration
camp in January 1945, aged 63

Suzanne MELOT died in
Ravensbrück concentration
camp in February 1945, aged 26

Chevalier Eric de MENTEN de
HORNES was shot in Brussels
on 20 October 1943, aged 28

Albert MEUNIER was executed
in Wolfenbüttel concentration
camp on 7 June 1944, aged 46

Victor MICHIELS was killed in
Brussels on 19 November 1942,
aged 26

Jean MOBERS was shot in
Ludwigsburg on 19 April 1944,
aged 29

Octave MONDO was shot in
Ludwigsburg on 30 June 1944,
aged 47

Suzanne MONDO died in
Ravensbrück concentration
camp on 29 April 1945, aged 48

Ernest van MOORLEGHEM was
shot in Bayreuth concentration
camp on 29 November 1944,
aged 29

Gertrude MOORS died in
Ravensbrück concentration
camp on 5 May 1945, aged 42

Hector MOREAU died in Gross-Rosen concentration camp on 18 December 1944, aged 55

Charles MORELLE died in Dachau concentration camp on 18 May 1945, aged 30

Emile NELIS died in Sonnenburg concentration camp in June 1944, aged 57

Zélia NELIS died in Ravensbrück concentration camp in May 1945, aged 56

Henri NEURAY died in the Saint Gilles Prison, Brussels, on 1 May 1944, aged 39

Ghislain NEYBERGH was shot in Brussels on 20 October 1943, aged 33

Maurice OLDERS died in Ellrich concentration camp on 11 December 1944, aged 57

Fernande ONIMUS died in Ravensbrück concentration camp in April 1945, aged 45

Père Henri van OSTAYEN died in Bergen-Belsen concentration camp on 19 April 1945, aged 39

Fernande OTTEN disappeared in Ravensbrück concentration camp after his arrest in 1942, aged 50

Isabelle PAULI died in the Belzig concentration camp on 29 September 1944, aged 58

Fernand PETITJEAN died on his return from Germany on 13 July 1945, aged 54

Arsinoé PHARAZYN died in Oranienburg concentration camp in 1944–45, aged 49

Victor PHARAZYN died in Neuengamme concentration camp on 29 February 1945, aged 45

Emilie PIGUET died in Ravensbrück concentration camp in 1944–45, aged 53

Hélène PILATTE died in Ravensbrück concentration camp in February 1945, aged 45

Valentine PLOYART died in Waldheim on 2 April 1945, aged 35

André POLAIN died in Siegburg concentration camp on 8 June 1944, aged 27

Léopold PRIEST was killed on 1 July 1944, aged 28

André RAFFALOVICH died in Buchenwald concentration camp in 1944–45, aged 48

Antoine RENAUD was shot in Brussels on 20 October 1943, aged 52

William REYNOLDS was executed in Brandenburg on 24 January 1944, aged 53

Robert ROBERTS JONES was shot in Brussels on 20 October 1943, aged 50

Jean ROCHER died at Dora on 27 October 1944, aged 39

Simone SAINTE-BEUVE died in Bergen-Belsen concentration camp in May 1945, aged 44

André SANTUS died in Fallersleben concentration camp on 8 January 1945, aged 48

Lucien SCHALENBORGH died in Halle Prison on 4 February 1945, aged 40

Paul SCHOENMACKERS died in Oberitz on 21 April 1945, aged 58

Gérald SCHRADER died in Ellrich concentration camp in 1944–45, aged 20

Théodore SCHRADER died in Nordhausen concentration camp on 23 July 1944, aged 55

Victor SCHREYEN died in Buchenwald concentration camp in 1944–45, aged 28

Lambert SPANOGHE was shot in Ludwigsburg on 30 June 1944, aged 44

Louise STASSART died in Ravensbrück concentration camp on 25 February 1945, aged 57

François STRENS disappeared in Sonnenburg concentration camp after being arrested in 1941, aged 40

Jean-Baptiste SUGG died in Kuselitz on 5 May 1945, aged 47

Elise TEDESCO died in Berlin from effects of captivity in May 1945, aged 29

Gilbert TEDESCO died in Breendonck in 1944–45, aged 36

Marie-Rose THIBAUT disappeared near Rechlin on 15 March 1945, aged 32

Marcelle THIERRY died in Ravensbrück concentration camp on 9 February 1945, aged 59

Jacques TINEL died in Mittelbau-Dora concentration camp on 19 December 1943, aged 23

Comte Antoine d'URSEL drowned while crossing the Bidassoa on 24 December 1943, aged 47

Francia USANDIZANGA died in Ravensbrück concentration camp on 12 April 1945, aged 36

Joseph VAEREWYCK died at Siegburg on 18 June 1942, aged 42

Roger VANDERHOEFT died in Ellrich concentration camp on 15 January 1945, aged 41

Odile VERHULST died in Ravensbrück concentration camp on 20 February 1945, aged 63

Edouard VERPRAET was shot on 20 October 1943, aged 48

Mathilde VERSPYCK died in Ravensbrück concentration camp on 11 May 1945, aged 36

Marie VIGNOL disappeared after being condemned to death in 1942, aged 44

Guillaume van WAMBEKE died in Germany in April 1945, aged 32

Marguerite WIGREN disappeared in Germany in 1944–45, aged 33

Valentin YARMONKINE disappeared in Germany in 1944–45, aged 46